3 4028 06912 4643
HARRIS COUNTY PUBLIC LIBRARY

200.973 Sta
Stark, Rodney
What Americans really
  believe : new findings
  from the Baylor surveys
                      $24.95
          ocn191924243
          11/26/2008

What American

WITHDRAWN

WHAT AMERICANS REALLY BELIEVE

New Findings from the Baylor Surveys of Religion

Rodney Stark

with

Christopher Bader, Joseph Baker, Kevin Dougherty, Scott Draper,
Robyn Driskell, Paul Froese, Carl R. Gwin, Sung Joon Jang,
Byron Johnson, Megan Johnson, Jordan LaBouff, Larry Lyon,
Carson Mencken, Charles M. North, Wafa Hakim Orman,
Ashley Palmer-Boyes, Jerry Z. Park, and Wade Rowatt

BAYLOR UNIVERSITY PRESS

© 2008 by Baylor University Press
Waco, Texas 76798

All Rights Reserved. No part of this publication may be reproduced, stored in a retrieval system, or transmitted, in any form or by any means, electronic, mechanical, photocopying, recording or otherwise, without the prior permission in writing of Baylor University Press.

Cover Design by Nicole Weaver, Zeal Design
Cover Photo: Urban scene with cathedral and skyscrapers, New York City. Photograph by Sven Hagolani. Used by permission of Getty Images.

All author's royalties from this book will be donated to the Institute for Studies of Religion.

Library of Congress Cataloging-in-Publication Data

Stark, Rodney.
  What Americans really believe : new findings from the Baylor surveys of religion / Rodney Stark with Christopher Bader ... [et al.].
       p. cm.
  Includes bibliographical references.
  ISBN 978-1-60258-178-4 (pbk. : alk. paper)
  1. United States--Religion--1960- I. Title.

BL2525.S725 2008
200.973'090511--dc22
                                        2008022188

CONTENTS

Part III
Atheism and Irreligion

Part IV
The Public Square

Introduction
The Stability and Diversity of American Faith

Forty years ago, results from the first two major surveys ever done of American religious beliefs and practices were published in *American Piety.*[*] For the very first time it was possible to examine many aspects of our national religious life: Who prays, when, and why? Do many Americans expect the second coming of Jesus, and how soon? Are mystical experiences rare events? How many people have changed their religious affiliations, and what are the denominational trends? Who gives how much money to their church? What must one do to be saved? How many people watch religious television (then in its infancy)? Who reads the Bible? The survey addressed these and dozens of other questions about religion that had never been asked before.

In pursuit of answers to these questions, the authors conducted two opinion surveys. One was based on a random sample of persons listed on the membership rolls of Christian churches in four counties in the San Francisco Bay Area. The data were collected in 1963. The other survey was based on a random sample of American adults, conducted by the National Opinion Research Center of the University of Chicago in October 1964.

---

* Rodney Stark and Charles Y. Glock, *American Piety: The Nature of Religious Commitment* (Berkeley: University of California Press, 1968).

1

Although the authors were pleased by enthusiastic responses to the surveys in *American Piety* from the media as well as from other researchers, they assumed that their findings merely marked the beginning of research on American faith—that many expanded and more sophisticated studies would soon follow. This proved to be much too optimistic. George Gallup Jr.[1] did use his famous polling agency to survey religious topics from time to time, and when he wasn't busy writing best-selling mystery novels, Andrew Greeley[2] did the same at the National Opinion Research Center. Aside from this work, the few national studies that gave any attention to religion, such as the General Social Surveys, did little more than repeat several of the questions first used in *American Piety*. Hence, rather than expanding the range of topics, many important matters included in the initial surveys were ignored. For example, the whole topic of salvation disappeared; almost nothing was ever asked again about prayer; the social aspects of congregational life were ignored; and it was twenty-five years before anyone is known to have asked again about church contributions.

So, more than forty years after the original studies were conducted, the Baylor Surveys of Religion were instituted to take up where *American Piety* left off. The first national Baylor survey was conducted in the fall of 2005, and the sample included 1,721 adults. The second survey was made in the fall of 2007 and the sample included 1,648 adults. A third national survey, focused on economics and religion, was conducted in the spring of 2006 and 1,032 adults were in the sample. All three surveys were carried out by the Gallup Organization under contract to Baylor's Institute for Studies of Religion (www.isreligion.org). The research was supported by grants from the John Templeton Foundation.

This volume was written to highlight some of the new findings and new topics. However, this opening chapter is devoted to connecting our recent findings with those of forty years ago (and longer) as a demonstration of the two most important aspects of American religious life: *stability* and *diversity*. That is, Americans differ greatly in their religious tastes and convictions, and these differences are remarkably durable.

PREDICTING THE END OF DENOMINATIONALISM

During the 1950s it became the received wisdom that denominationalism was no longer a significant factor among American Protestants. The argument was made that because the various Protestant bodies had originated primarily in the different ethnic origins of Americans, as ethnicity had faded in importance, there was little reason for Lutherans to be divided from Episcopalians or Presbyterians from Baptists. As Will Herberg put it in a best-selling book, Americans now shared a "common religion" that was only moderately separable into three groups: Protestants, Catholics, and Jews.[3] So many denominational leaders and professors at the elite divinity schools were convinced that a "common core Protestantism" had emerged in America, they assumed that church unity was not only desirable, but inevitable. Efforts to bring this about were known as the ecumenical movement, and many interdenominational conversations were initiated in pursuit of denominational mergers. That these mergers would surely happen seemed so certain that a well-known seminary professor published a book to explain ahead of time why the reunification of Protestantism had taken place.[4] Some regretted this impending change.[5] But everyone believed it was certain to happen.

Although standing on the sidelines, the leading sociologists of religion of that time also supported the claims that a religious consensus had been achieved and took that for granted in their research. Thus, a much-praised study examined the effects of American religion on politics, economic success, and family life without paying any attention to Protestant denominational differences, or even to variations in the intensity of an individual's religiousness. Rather, Gerhard Lenski defined the "religious factor" as nothing more than religious preference and devoted his efforts merely to comparing Protestants, Catholics, and Jews.[6] At the time, no reviewer objected.

The fundamental assumption of this whole perspective was that the traditional doctrines of Christianity had lost their credibility, and therefore American religion was rapidly shifting "from a literalistic old-time faith to demythologized modernism."[7]

Perhaps the most remarkable fact was that all these assumptions about religious change were based on the impressions of "experts," none of whom had seen any data on what people in the churches did or didn't believe. Worse yet, these "experts" were mostly based in the elite, very liberal divinity schools, where they were isolated and insulated from ordinary believers. All they knew for certain was what they no longer believed.

Then came *American Piety* offering actual data on what Americans believed. Most of the "experts" were stunned into silence, and a few even changed their minds when they saw tables such as this one.

Table 1
Faith in Jesus (Christian church-member sample, 1963)

	Jesus was born of a virgin	Jesus will actually return to earth some day
	"completely true"	"definitely"
United Church of Christ	21%	13%
Methodist	34%	21%
Episcopal	39%	24%
Disciples of Christ	62%	36%
Presbyterian	57%	43%
American Lutheran	66%	54%
American Baptist	69%	57%
Missouri Lutheran	92%	75%
Southern Baptist	99%	94%
Small evangelical bodies	96%	89%
Total Protestant	57%	44%
Roman Catholic	81%	47%

Clearly, traditional Christian beliefs, at least those concerning Jesus, had been fading away in *some* denominations. Only very small minorities in the United Church of Christ fully accepted the virgin birth and the second coming, and firm belief in these matters was also in the minority among Methodists and Episcopalians. But an overwhelming and unflinching commitment to tradition remained in others—more than 90 percent of Southern Baptists stood firm, even while living in the San Francisco Bay Area. As a result, rather than having become irrelevant, denominationalism had become more profoundly important than ever before in history. Where once the denominations were separated mostly by ethnic origins or by theological quibbles, now they were sundered over the most fundamental of all Christian beliefs, those concerning the divinity of Christ.

Lest anyone think that the disputes were limited to Jesus or that the findings shown in Table 1 were peculiar to church members in the San Francisco Bay Area, *American Piety* was filled with similar findings based on a survey of the entire nation—as can be seen in Table 2.

This table includes all the people who merely reported a religious preference, many of whom did not actually participate in that or any denomination, along with the real members. That explains why the level of belief is lower here than in Table 1. But the overall conclusion remains the same: denominational differences within Protestantism were huge. It is no wonder that the ecumenical movement went nowhere.

Far more important is the fact that, as noted by the authors of *American Piety*, the denominations that still sustained traditional faith were the ones that were growing. And grow they did. Several of those included in the "small" group back in 1963–1964, such as the Church of God in Christ and the Assemblies of God, have become major bodies, the former now having 5.7 million members and the latter 2.7 million. Meanwhile, the denominations where "demythologized modernism" had made substantial headway all suffered catastrophic declines. Taking population

TABLE 2

The Devil and Life beyond Death (National sample, 1964)

	"Absolutely sure there is a devil"	"Absolutely sure there is life beyond death"
Unitarian	0%	0%
United Church of Christ	7%	26%
United Presbyterian	20%	36%
Protestant Episcopal	21%	35%
The Christian Church	29%	42%
Methodist	33%	42%
Presbyterian Church U.S.	35%	43%
American Lutheran bodies	31%	52%
Evangelical Reform	39%	50%
Lutheran, Missouri Synod	44%	50%
American Baptist	47%	41%
Other Baptist bodies	55%	59%
Southern Baptist	55%	65%
Small evangelical bodies	61%	67%
Total Protestant	40%	50%
Roman Catholic	36%	48%

growth into account, between 1960 and 2000, the United Church of Christ declined by 60 percent, the Episcopal Church by 55 percent, the Methodists by 49 percent, the Presbyterians by 45 percent, and the Lutherans by 39 percent. Meanwhile, the Assemblies of God grew by 225 percent, and the Church of God in Christ by nearly 800 percent. Even the enormous Southern Baptist Convention managed to grow by 5 percent during this period.[8]

In the past several years liberal church leaders and sociologists have once again been proclaiming the end of denominationalism. A leading proponent is Robert Wuthnow, whose *The Restructuring of American Religion* is cited by everyone as "proof" that denominationalism has declined. As he put it: "over the past half-century denominationalism has declined seriously as the primary mode of identification in American religion."[9] Wuthnow bases his claim on the fact that members of the various denominations are about equally opposed or favorable to various social issues such as abortion and premarital sex. He also makes much of the existence of many nondenominational special-purpose religious groups—although he fails to show that this really is anything new (as compared with the abolition or prohibition eras) or how such groups diminish the importance of denominations.

No one would deny that the decline in the importance of ethnicity has affected Protestantism, at least to the extent that what used to be six Lutheran churches (the Norwegian, Swedish, Danish, Finnish, Icelandic, and German) managed to unite. Nor could anyone doubt that evangelical Protestantism is somewhat transdenominational in that there have arisen some evangelical congregations that are without denominational ties. It may even be that Evangelicals today may shift from one specific denominational body to another more easily than their parents did (although American rates of denominational shifting always have been very high).

That being said, consider Table 3. Two things stand out. First, denominationalism is alive. Second, the percentages expressing certainty in these two beliefs have risen in *every* denomination since 1964. That could have occurred because many of the nontraditional believers present in the "liberal" denominations back in 1963–1964 ended up leaving the churches—as reflected in the declining membership of these groups. This did not lead to a decline in traditional belief among the general public, nor did it inflate the proportion of the unchurched, because many of the defectors' sons and daughters returned to the churches. This is supported by data showing that the majority of Americans raised in irreligious homes end up joining a religious group, most often one with a traditional theology.[10]

TABLE 3
Satan and Heaven (Baylor Survey, 2005)

	Satan "absolutely exists"	Heaven "absolutely exists"
Unitarian	11%	17%
United Church of Christ	25%	36%
Episcopalian	41%	54%
Methodist	57%	74%
Presbyterian	60%	75%
Lutheran	60%	71%
All Liberal Protestants*	52%	66%
Church of God in Christ	77%	79%
Pentecostal	91%	83%
Baptist	92%	94%
Assemblies of God	98%	100%
All Conservative Protestants*	88%	92%
Latter-day Saints (Mormon)	87%	98%
Roman Catholic	52%	69%
Jewish	8%	27%

* Including denominations not shown separately above.

DECLINING ATTENDANCE

Whatever else may have taken place in American religious life, it is widely agreed that rates of church attendance have dropped substantially over the past forty years. In *Bowling Alone*, Harvard political scientist Robert D. Putnam claimed church attendance fell rapidly during the 1960s and continues to slide downward.[11] Even such a prominent sociologist of religion as Robert Wuthnow sings in this choir: "Church attendance also turned downward. After peaking in 1958 at around 49 percent (people who said they had been to a religious service within the past week), it declined steadily.

. . ."[12] Putnam may have written in ignorance, but Wuthnow must have known full well what this "decline" really reflected.

Until the middle 1960s, Roman Catholic church-attendance rates were nearly double those of Protestants, mainly because the church defined deliberately missing Mass as a sin requiring penance. Thus, the *American Piety* national survey done in 1964 found that 68 percent of Catholics and 35 percent of Protestants claimed to attend church every week. Then in 1967 the famous Vatican II Council decided that it no longer was a sin for Catholics to miss Mass. As would be expected, this relaxation of the rules resulted in many Catholics going to Mass less often than every week. Today Catholics attend church at about the same rate as Protestants (see chap. 1). Consequently, as compared with the days before the council's declaration, the overall rate of American church attendance declined. But that is it. There has been no other decline in church attendance in the past fifty years, as is shown in Table 4.

TABLE 4
Weekly Church Attendance, 1954–2005

	Attend weekly
1954 (Gallup)	44%
1968 (Gallup)	45%
1964 (*American Piety*)	44%
Catholics no longer required to attend every week	
1973 (GSS*)	36%
1975 (GSS)	36%
1980 (GSS)	35%
1985 (GSS)	37%
1990 (GSS)	35%
1998† (GSS)	32%
2005 (Baylor)	38%
2007 (Baylor)	36%

* General Social Survey
† No GSS in 1995

What a remarkable example of stability as the differences across the years are well within the random variation of samples this size. But somehow, American intellectuals, even those whose business it is to know about trends in American religion, just can't accept that religion isn't on its way out.

"Losing Our Young People"

Publication of a finding about age and church attendance by the Barna Group in 2006 ignited a great deal of concern in America's churches. Sermon after sermon was devoted to the crisis of faith that was turning millions of young people away from church. Groups of concerned clergy announced plans for special campaigns aimed at recovering "our lost young people." Sophisticated observers blamed all of the usual cultural suspects, from sex-drenched media to rock-and-roll. Some even blamed the churches (especially the evangelical churches) for serving up shallow theology.[13]

Table 5 reveals the cause of all the panic. These data are from the Baylor survey, not from the Barna Group, but the results are the same: the younger they are, the less likely Americans are to attend church.

TABLE 5	
Age and Church Attendance (Baylor Survey, 2005)	
	Never attend church
18–29	28%
30–39	25%
Over 40	20%

But the concern generated by this finding is a false alarm. This same effect can be found in *every* national survey of church attendance ever done. Young people have always been less likely to attend than are older people.

Does this mean that youth have been defecting from the churches decade after decade? Writing in 1976, Robert Wuthnow seems to have thought so.[14] But if that were true, studies should not continue to reveal an increase in church attendance as the people under thirty in one sample year move into the older age groups in later studies. What this persistent finding actually reveals is far more mundane than the notion that young people are leaving the churches. It merely shows that when young people leave home, some of them tend to sleep in on Sunday morning rather than go to church. That they haven't defected is obvious from the fact that a bit later in life when they have married, and especially after children arrive, they become more regular attenders. This happens every generation.

However, clearly some denominations *are* losing their young adults—not to irreligion, but to other denominations, as evident in the fact that some denominations are rapidly shrinking while others are rapidly growing.

Church Membership: 1776–2005

Maybe religion isn't on its way out, but it certainly is far less influential and universal than it used to be. Robert Wuthnow claims that the percentage of the American population that belongs to a church has long been declining.[15] And, obviously, no American community today can generate the level of piety that prevailed in the Massachusetts Bay Colony or in Quaker Philadelphia in, say, 1776. Wrong. Church membership today is far higher than it was in colonial times, and Robert Wuthnow to the contrary, the membership rate has been rising for more than two hundred years.

In 1776 on the average weekend there were more people in the Boston taverns on Saturday night than turned up in church on Sunday morning. And there weren't all that many Quakers in Pennsylvania—there were a lot more Presbyterians and members of the German Reformed Church. But the overwhelming majority, not only in Pennsylvania or in Massachusetts but in all of the colonies, belonged to no church at all.

In *The Churching of America, 1776–1990*, the authors[16] reconstructed church membership rates, beginning in 1776 and ending in 1990. Although the procedures involved in these calculations were quite elaborate, they have generally been acknowledged as adequate. And probably the most surprising result was that only about 17 percent of Americans actually belonged to a church in 1776. Keep in mind that in any era, including now, many people will name a religious preference if asked (nearly 90 percent of Americans do so today), but many of these people do not actually maintain a membership in any specific congregation. The reason the book's title refers to the *churching* of America is because through the past two centuries Americans have become far more churched—an increasingly higher percentage actually belong to a local congregation.

TABLE 6

Percent of Americans Who Belong to a Local Congregation

1776	17%
1850	34%
1860	37%
1870	35%
1890	45%
1906	51%
1916	53%
1926	56%
1952	59%
1980	62%
1990	64%
2005*	69%

* From the Baylor survey[17]

What a remarkable change. Church membership has risen from about 17 percent to almost 70 percent.

How did this happen? Why has American church membership risen for more than two hundred years? In a word, denominationalism. Or more specifically, the need to compete with other groups for members in order to sustain themselves generates energetic churches that collectively maximize the religious recruitment of a population.

One of the most common myths about religion is that people in medieval Europe were devout worshipers. Instead, faced with a lazy, monopoly church supported by taxes, medieval Europeans as a whole were remarkable for their lack of religious participation. Then, following the Reformation, the Protestants quickly established monopoly state churches in northern Europe and England that were, if anything, even less energetic than the Catholic churches of southern Europe. For example, in England, the Oxford Diocesan Visitations of 1738 found that fewer than 5 percent of the total population had taken part in Communion the previous year—although such participation was required by law.[18]

Settlers coming to America brought these European habits of little religious participation with them—Puritans were never more than a small minority; they weren't even a majority of those aboard the *Mayflower*. This is reflected in the fact that only 17 percent of Americans belonged to a church in 1776.

Keep in mind that in 1776 there were tax-supported, established churches in most of the colonies: the Congregationalists in New England and the Anglicans most everywhere else. But the appearance of Baptists and Methodists and then a host of other upstart sects soon changed the whole picture. Consequently, by the middle of the nineteenth century about a third of Americans belonged to a local church. The small decline for 1870 reflects the social disorganization of the South after the Civil War. By the turn of the twentieth century the halfway mark had been reached, and the percentages have risen slowly ever since.

That this achievement is the result of competition among religious bodies in search of members is demonstrated by the fact that as denominations have ceased to pursue new members, they have rapidly declined, with corresponding growth by those bodies that continue to seek members—as will be seen in chapter 2.

Conclusion

The issues pursued in this chapter demonstrate the stability of American religion. Denominationalism persists as a major phenomenon. Church attendance has held rock steady, except for the entirely understandable decline in Catholic attendance. In each generation, young people are poorer attenders than are those a bit older. But American religion also is very diverse. Many people believe many different things. This is both a cause and a consequence of denominations, as groups have arisen to meet these different preferences. But perhaps the most remarkable consequence of American denominationalism is to have created such a high level of religious mobilization. The great majority of Americans belong to a church and attend with some frequency.

These examples also reveal how often even very reputable observers of American religion get things wrong and some of the potential costs of their errors. For example, it would be a waste of their funds for some churches to mount a campaign to save their young people from leaving the church, when no such thing is going on. On the other hand, some groups clearly are losing their young (and many of their older members too), not to irreligion but to other denominations. For these churches, any effort to reverse their declines depends upon being able to motivate their current members to reach out to others.

Thus, an important reason for doing the Baylor surveys is to accurately portray the realities and trends in our religious life. In doing so, the chapters that follow will reveal many other misperceptions about American religion, repeatedly finding examples of stability and diversity.

PART 1

CONGREGATIONS

CHURCH-GOING
Labels Matter

I n recent years there have been a number of attempts made to
minimize the actual rate of church attendance in America,
some of them remarkably impassioned (one of the more prominent proponents of this claim actually broke into sobs when his
views were questioned at an academic meeting). No one disputes
that a significant number of Americans who tell pollsters that they
go to church *every* Sunday, probably only go *most* Sundays and
therefore that the consistent finding that about 35 percent are in
church any given Sunday is a bit high. Of course, those determined to "prove" that America isn't really as religious as it is made
out to be and that faith is rapidly fading away are given to even
greater exaggerations than the public when they suggest that the
true rate of church attendance is well below 20 percent.[1]

More careful studies by more qualified researchers suggest
that the overstatement of church attendance is quite small, being
only about 1.1 times the actual rate of attendance, so the average rate probably is around 31 or 32 percent.[2] Of course, as has
been well documented, attendance varies by the weather and the
season.[3]

In addition to claims that church attendance "really" is
low and declining, many are the claims and tacit assumptions

TABLE 7

Income, Education, and Church Attendance

Annual family income	Attend weekly
$20,000 or less	38%
$20,000 to $50,000	36%
$50,000 to $100,000	39%
$100,000 to $150,000	38%
Over $150,000	31%
Education	
High school or less	40%
Attended college	38%
College graduate	37%
Postgraduate	39%

that, of course, intelligent, well-educated, affluent folks seldom attend—that the folks in the pews on Sunday overwhelmingly are poor, uneducated failures. That's easy to check out.

So much for these myths. As we see in Table 7 income has no apparent impact on church attendance, with the possible exception that those with incomes over $150,000 are a bit less likely to attend. As for education, there is no effect at all: those with postgraduate training are as likely to attend church as are those whose education ended at high school or sooner.

While it is true that more conservative denominations generate high rates of weekly attendance, the differences are not huge—most groups have quite good levels of attendance, as Table 8 indicates.

What else influences attendance?

• *Gender*: Women (44%) attend more than do men (32%).

• *Race*: African Americans (46%) attend at a higher rate than whites (37%).

• *Marital Status*: Widows (who mostly are older women) are the best attenders (53%), followed by married people (44%), while the

TABLE 8
Denomination and Church Attendance

	Attend weekly
Unitarian	7%
United Church of Christ	27%
Lutheran	32%
Methodist	36%
Episcopalian	41%
Presbyterian	46%
All Liberal Protestants	36%
Pentecostal	48%
Baptist	53%
Assemblies of God	61%
All Conservative Protestants	54%
Roman Catholic	41%
Latter-day Saints (Mormon)	85%
Jewish	13%

divorced (21%) and those living together, but unmarried (10%), have the lowest level of attendance.

• *Age:* As noted in the introduction, people under 30 are most likely to never attend, but they are not less likely to attend weekly. Only people over 60 differ in terms of their frequency of attendance—48 percent attend weekly.

• *Politics:* Those who voted for George W. Bush in 2004 are far more likely (49%) to attend weekly than are Kerry voters (27%) or those who favored Ralph Nader (18%).

• *Region:* Not surprisingly, attendance is higher in the South (45%) and Midwest (41%) and lower in the West (33%) and East (32%).

CONCLUSION

Why are Americans such frequent church attenders? For the same reason that such a high proportion belong to a church: denominationalism. As was discussed in the introduction, the singular thing about American religion is an unregulated religious economy free from the stifling effects of a lazy, state-supported church—American churches must recruit or perish. The result is that literally tens of millions of Americans are on the look out to recruit new people for their congregations and work hard to keep them coming back once they have started to attend.

CHURCH GROWTH
Competing for Members

Early in 2008, when the Pew Forum on Religion and Public Life reported that 44 percent of American adults have switched from one denomination to another, many observers seemed to think this observation was a bit scandalous. The editors of the *Wall Street Journal* opined: "There are reasons to find this statistic troubling. People who leave one denomination for another may be more concerned with fulfilling their boutique church-going desires than with meeting the moral obligations of a religious group or the demands of a doctrine."[1]

Wrong. If that were true, then the more permissive "liberal" denominations would be gaining and the more demanding "conservative" denominations would be shrinking. In fact, as is obvious in Table 9, the "liberals" are declining so rapidly that their continued existence may be in question, while the conservative bodies are growing at a breakneck pace. Americans mostly change churches in search of a deeper, more compelling faith.

Instead of using simple membership totals, Table 9 is based on members per 1,000 U.S. population in order to take population growth into account. Another way to think of this membership data is as each group's "market share" in each of the two years. All of the liberal denominations have a shrinking market share,

TABLE 9

Some Growing and Some Declining American Denominations

	Members per 1,000 U.S. population		
	1960	2000	% Change
Christian Church (Disciples)	10.0	2.7	-71
United Church of Christ	12.4	5.0	-60
Episcopal Church	18.1	8.2	-55
United Methodist Church	58.9	29.8	-49
Presbyterian Church (USA)	23.0	12.7	-45
Evangelical Lutheran Church	29.3	18.2	-39
Unitarian-Universalist	1.0	0.8	-20
Liberal Protestants	*152.7*	*77.4*	*-49*
Southern Baptist Convention	53.8	56.3	+5
Church of the Nazarene	1.7	2.2	+35
Seventh-day Adventist	1.8	3.1	+72
Foursquare Gospel	0.5	0.9	+80
Jehovah's Witnesses*	1.4	3.5	+150
Assemblies of God	2.8	9.1	+225
Church of God (Cleveland, TN)	0.9	3.1	+244
Church of God in Christ	2.2	19.5	+786
Conservative Protestants	*73.3*	*115.9*	*+158*
Roman Catholic	233.0	221.7	-5
Latter-day Saints (Mormon)†	8.2	18.2	+122

* "Publishers" only
† American members only

Source: Calculated from the *Yearbook of American Churches, 1962* and *Yearbook of American and Canadian Churches, 2001*.

whereas all of the conservative bodies, including the very large Southern Baptist Convention, have grown very significantly over this forty-year period.

Of course, neither growth nor decline could have taken place unless some people departed from the church into which they were born and enrolled in another body. And the remarkable rates of growth and decline shown in Table 9 required that large numbers of people switch churches—the 44 percent that the Pew Forum reported.

However, there is nothing new about such extensive church-switching in America. In 1776 the Congregationalists were by far the largest denomination in the colonies. Today they are a minor denomination renamed the United Church of Christ. In 1776 the Methodists had just begun to grow, but a century later theirs was by far the largest denomination in America. Then, starting in the second half of the twentieth century, the Methodists entered a continuing period of serious decline. In contrast, back in 1960 the Assemblies of God and the Church of God in Christ were obscure evangelical Protestant bodies. Today they count their membership in the millions and continue their rapid growth. Anyone who thinks these are the less demanding and more fashionable religious boutiques is out of touch.

Why do so many people change churches, and why do most of them favor the more demanding denominations? Because American pluralism forces denominations to compete for members, and the more demanding denominations are far more effective competitors. Put another way, religious switching reflects the fundamental vigor of American religious life and the constant weeding out of ineffective religious denominations. This was well known in the nineteenth century when a whole series of European observers of the high levels of religious participation in the United States attributed it to competition. As the Viennese scholar Francis Grund put it in 1837, "Not only have Americans a greater number of clergymen than, in proportion to the population, can be found either on the Continent or in England; but they have not one idler amongst them; all being obliged to exert themselves for the spiritual welfare of their respective congregations."[2]

Unfortunately, this obvious fact was rejected during most of the twentieth century by both theologians and sociologists. The theologians (at least those in the more liberal seminaries) frequently condemned the existence of multiple denominations as a scandal and an affront to God and initiated many proposals for mergers. The sociologists stressed that pluralism was extremely harmful to faith and that competition among faiths would soon lead to secularization—the disappearance of religion from modern societies.

Beginning with the French sociologist Émile Durkheim, who taught that society itself is the real object of all religious worship, sociologists developed the thesis that the basic function of religion is to legitimate the norms of a society, to provide a common set of ideas, rituals, and symbols which can "provide an overarching sense of unity even in a society riddled with conflicts."[3] Peter Berger captured the essence of this claim when he used the term "Sacred Canopy" to identify this overarching and unifying religious aspect of all societies.[4] But, according to Berger, all "Sacred Canopies" are precarious and doomed if several religions compete within a society, for then the disagreements among faiths are mutually discrediting. That is, while each faith claims to have the truth, since they disagree, not all of them can be true, a disjunction which soon leads people to suppose that none can be true.

The idea that pluralism destroys the credibility of a society's "Sacred Canopy" helped justify the idea that religion must soon die out in modern, complex societies—a claim known as the *secularization thesis*. None of these sociologists was able to see that pluralism resulted in much more effective and successful religious organizations. Nor could any of these sociologists or, indeed, the many seminary professors who agreed with them,[5] grasp the possibility that it was the most "modernized" and undemanding faiths that would be unable to cope with competition. But that's what happened. By now even Peter Berger has dismissed the secularization thesis as misconceived, and no one can deny that it is the very conservative churches that are booming. This was not so evident in

TABLE 10
Denomination and Witnessing

"How often in the last month did you participate in witnessing/sharing your faith with strangers?"

	Once or more in past month
Pentecostal	70%
Assemblies of God	43%
Baptist	40%
All Conservative Protestants	*44%*
United Church of Christ	0%
Unitarian	3%
Lutheran	17%
Methodist	28%
Presbyterian	17%
All Liberal Protestants	*19%*
Roman Catholic	22%
Latter-day Saints (Mormon)	49%
Jewish	3%

the early 1960s, and while the authors of *American Piety* recognized that many Americans had switched churches, their samples were too small to allow them to correctly trace the direction of those changes.

Why do conservative churches outperform the liberals? Because they work much harder at attracting and holding members. How do they do that? By inspiring their members to witness to others.

Keep in mind that the categories "Lutheran," "Methodist," and "Presbyterian" include many separate denominations, some relatively large and quite conservative, and this inflates their witnessing. Even so, there are marked differences that clearly reveal an important reason why the conservative churches are growing: most church growth is the result of rank-and-file members bringing in new members.

In addition:

• *Gender*: Males and females were equally likely to witness.

• *Race*: African Americans (55%) were more likely than whites (28%) to witness.

• *Region*: Southerners were more likely to witness than were other Americans, but this was entirely due to differences in racial composition.

• *Age*: There was no significant age effect.

• *Politics*: Party preference was unrelated to witnessing.

• *Education*: People who did not enter college (34%) and those who attended college (33%) were equally likely to witness, but those who attended graduate school (16%) were much less likely to do so. This may be partly due to the fact that the graduate-educated were more likely than others to agree with the statement: "I have kept my religious beliefs to myself for fear of ridicule." A university faculty lounge would be a very uncomfortable place to do any witnessing.

Granted that church switching is symptomatic of religious discontent, the fact that nearly all who leave one denomination settle into another would seem to indicate that they found satisfaction elsewhere.

There is suggestive evidence that most Americans have found a satisfying religious affiliation. In the most recent Baylor Survey of American Religion, conducted by the Gallup Organization late in 2007, a large sample of American adults was asked to agree or disagree with the statement: "My life has real purpose." Overwhelmingly, Americans believe their lives have real purpose: 84 percent agreed. Of perhaps even greater significance is that there are no important denominational differences: Unitarians and Methodists were as likely to agree as were Mormons and Pentecostals. In that sense, everyone's current denomination seems to be a satisfactory "fit." In fact, only atheists fell well below the average, and even 64 percent of them said their lives have "real purpose."

If pluralism greatly increases the general level of religiousness by satisfying the diverse religious tastes of the public, it has two other consequences. It strengthens religious freedom and it promotes religious civility.

Political philosophy played little or no role in the decision of the Constitutional Convention to not designate an established church. At the time there were tax-supported, established churches in most of the colonies and many of the philosophers admired by the Founders, including Thomas Hobbes and David Hume, claimed that permitting several religions to exist in a society was asking for no end of conflict. The Founders opted for pluralism and later adopted the First Amendment prohibiting establishment, out of necessity. Pluralism was the reality of early America—not even the Congregationalists came close to enrolling a majority. So the Founders chose the course recommended by Adam Smith, who proposed that the secret to religious peace was a society "divided into two or three hundred, or perhaps as many [as a] thousand small sects, of which no one could be considerable enough to disturb publick tranquillity."[6]

Smith also argued quite convincingly that the leaders of these many sects would necessarily learn to be respectful and agreeable toward one another, since each was surrounded on all sides by potential adversaries. Of course, effective norms of religious civility and tolerance have developed only slowly and inconsistently. Anti-Semitism has largely been laid to rest and so has anti-Catholicism. But, as has been evident in the 2008 presidential campaign, it is still regarded as acceptable to express nasty prejudice against Mormons and evangelical Christians. The media and the liberal establishment don't seem to care that the social, moral, and political views of Mormons and evangelical Christians are not very distinctive from those of most other Americans. It is enough that they are not in accord with the views held by avid listeners to National Public Radio. Hence, a recent national survey of college professors found that 53 percent of them admitted to having negative feelings toward Evangelicals and 33 percent had such feelings toward Mormons.[7]

Consistent with those findings, studies show that the most virulent and common form of religious intolerance still to be found in America is that held by the irreligious toward the religious.[8] As for the reverse, religious people express little hostility toward the irreligious, perhaps regarding them as too few to matter. It should be noted, however, that religious people do resent how they are portrayed by the media—54 percent of Mormons, 53 percent of Evangelicals, and 44 percent of Baptists (compared with 7 percent of Episcopalians) agree that "My religious beliefs are often ridiculed by the media."

CONCLUSION

In 1858 the militantly antireligious German writer Karl T. Griesinger noted that pluralism was responsible for the very high level of religiousness in the United States: "Clergymen in America [are] like other businessmen; they must meet competition and build up a trade, and it is their own fault if their income is not large enough. Now it is clear why Heaven and Hell are moved to drive the people to the churches, and why attendance is more common here than anywhere else in the world."[9] He was quite right. Competition is the central factor in the growth and decline of American denominations, and the combined efforts of the many separate religious organizations is the reason that church membership and religious participation are so much higher here than in Europe. Unlike Europeans, when Americans grow dissatisfied with their churches, rather than cease attending, they simply switch to a church that better satisfies them.

3

STRICT CHURCHES
The Reasons for Their Popularity

For many observers of the American religious scene, especially Europeans, the real mystery is why the strict churches—those that demand much of their members—are the ones that are flourishing, while the more permissive and accommodating churches are falling by the wayside. The previous chapter explained one aspect of this phenomenon by showing that the strict churches stimulate their members to greater outreach effort. But that does not explain why these outreach efforts are so successful. Why will people join and remain active in churches that demand more from them than do many other available options?

This phenomenon seems to violate the basic law of economics that, other things being equal, people will seek to minimize their costs. It does not actually violate this law, because other things are *not equal*—not all religious "goods" are of equivalent value. Many of the more "expensive" religious options yield such superior benefits that they are, for most people, the better buy. That is, strict churches grow because they give greater satisfaction to their members. In what follows, we will see why and how this is the case.

STRICTNESS AS TENSION

Strict religions are those that exist in a relatively high state of tension with their sociocultural environment—the extent to which religious groups "fit in" vis-à-vis secular society.[1] Some groups are so accepting of worldly norms, rules, and values as to be virtually indistinguishable from the surrounding culture. Sociologists often refer to such groups as "churches." "Sects," on the other hand, reject some aspects of the secular culture. As these two names imply, religious groups can be ordered along a continuum made up of the *degree of tension* between religious organizations and their sociocultural environments.[2] At one pole are very high tension groups that reject many aspects of conventional culture, and at the other pole are low-tension groups that are comfortable with nearly all aspects of the surrounding culture.

The 2007 Baylor Religion Survey included a series of items that make it possible to use respondent reports to assess the degree of tension between their church and the general culture. The survey asked respondents:

"By your best guess, how would your place of worship feel about the following?":

Pornography	Forbids 65%	Discourages 27%	Combined 92%
Abortion	Forbids 52%	Discourages 32%	Combined 84%
Homosexual behavior	Forbids 44%	Discourages 33%	Combined 77%
Premarital sex	Forbids 38%	Discourages 51%	Combined 89%
Living together	Forbids 32%	Discourages 53%	Combined 85%
Gambling	Forbids 22%	Discourages 60%	Combined 82%

Wearing revealing clothing	Forbids	Discourages	Combined
	13%	71%	84%

Nearly all respondents say their religious groups are against pornography, but relatively few forbid revealing clothing, although most discourage it. In fact, most people say their groups at least discourage each of these activities.

These seven items were summed to create an Index of Tension that was collapsed into four values from Low to High, with about 25 percent of the sample in each category. It will be adequate to contrast the highest with the lowest category. As would be expected, the Index is highly related to denomination.

TABLE 11
Denomination and Tension

	High tension	Low tension
Assemblies of God	81%	0%
Pentecostal	75%	0%
Baptist	49%	6%
All Conservative Protestants	53%	8%
Episcopalian	0%	78%
United Church of Christ	0%	67%
Presbyterian	8%	59%
Lutheran	12%	37%
Methodist	18%	35%
All Liberal Protestants	13%	47%
Roman Catholic	37%	10%
Latter-day Saints (Mormon)	94%	3%
Jewish	0%	83%
All Americans	35%	21%

Reading across the table, what these results show is that tension (or strictness) clearly separates Protestants into conservative and liberal groups, and that Roman Catholics tend to be more like Conservative Protestants, at least on these issues.

The question remains, why do people seem to prefer the more "costly" religious bodies—the ones that ask more of them? Imagine two churches. At one of them, every Sunday seems like a major holiday. The church is full and everyone helps to "make a joyful noise unto the Lord." The collection plates come back overflowing, and every week there are new people to welcome. Now imagine a church where there are good turnouts at Christmas and Easter, but on regular Sundays most of the pews are empty and budget problems are chronic. Other things being equal, it would be far more pleasant and rewarding to attend the full, active church.

TABLE 12
Tension and Church Participation

	High tension	Low tension
Attends weekly or more often	61%	20%
Attended Bible study or Sunday school during the past month	57%	18%
Attended a church social event during the past month	60%	43%
Attended choir practice or other musical programs during the past month	20%	10%

What is immediately apparent is the immense gulf between high and low tension groups in terms of participation, very much in keeping with our two imaginary churches. About one of five low-tension respondents reported attending church at least once a week, compared to nearly two-thirds of those in higher-tension groups. Higher tension respondents are also significantly more likely to engage in activities outside the regular service. They are nearly twice as likely as low-tension respondents to participate in the choir. They are more than three times as likely to attend Bible study or Sunday school. More than half report attending social gatherings with other members at least once a month.

Economist Laurence Iannaccone has offered some interesting insights as to why strict churches manifest so much higher levels of member participation.[3] As does any group, churches are forced to deal with what economists call the "free rider" problem. Some members would prefer to reap the benefits of belonging to a religious organization without having to give much in return. The stereotypical "Christmas Catholic" is the ultimate free rider, enjoying Christmas Mass once a year but avoiding services for the remainder. Much more common are members of a church who would like to attend on an occasional Sunday but who donate very little of their time or money to keep the church operating. Such free riders drain the resources of a group and the enthusiasm of other members. It is very hard for one to maintain a high level of commitment and participation when most other folks do not.

Iannaccone argues that one way that religious groups can reduce the number of free riders is to make costly demands upon members. Imposing requirements, forbidding certain behaviors, and so on make the cost of minimal participation outweigh the benefits to such an extent that people either get with it or get out. For example, one supposes that there would be a sharp decline in the number of Christmas Catholics should the church begin to take attendance and require that in order to remain a member, Catholics must attend at least once a month. No doubt, some Catholics would leave the church rather than meet that demand, but the example of the strict denominations suggests that many others would respond by becoming more active and that in the end the level of satisfaction on the part of the average Catholic would rise.

Since members of higher-tension groups spend more time together outside of the main service, we should expect them to develop tighter bonds. And indeed they do.

	High tension	Low tension
TABLE 13 *Tension and Friendship*		
How many of your friends:		
Attend your place of worship half or more of friends	43%	18%
Do not attend religious services half or more of friends	13%	30%

When asked how many of their friends attend their place of worship, 43 percent of high-tension respondents, compared with only 18 percent of low-tension respondents, reported that half or more of their friends were in their congregation. Members of higher-tension groups share the pews with friends. Those attending lower-tension churches are much more likely to be seated next to strangers or at least people they would not count amongst their friends. Indeed, low-tension respondents were almost twice as likely (30%) as were high-tension respondents (13%) to report that half or more of their friends don't go to any church.

All of this suggests that high-tension groups succeed simply because they provide a better "product." Members are more committed to the group and eager to show up on Sunday. Choirs are vibrant and engaged. Shared meals and get-togethers are frequent. Bonds of trust are built between members such that attendance on Sunday is a meeting of friends.

TENSION AND GROUP RESOURCES

If someone provides a better product, we typically assume that consumers will be willing to pay more for it. One way that people can "pay" for a product is through their time. We have already seen that higher-tension churches engender greater attendance, commitment, and bonding between members. The strength of a high-tension product also applies to funding.

	High tension	Low tension
Do you tithe?		
Yes	56%	20%
Average annual church contribution		
(rounded to nearest $100)	$2,000	$1,100
Contributed $5,000 or more		
in 2006	18%	4%

TABLE 14
Tension and Church Contributions

High-tension respondents are nearly three times (56%) as likely to tithe as are lower-tension respondents (20%). On average they also gave about twice as much money. Perhaps more telling are contributions to church as a percent of income. After all, a contribution of $2,000 means rather less to a person who makes $100,000 a year than it does to someone earning $40,000. Even by this measure, higher-tension respondents far outgive those of lower tension—on average, low-tension respondents give about 1.8 percent of their income to their churches compared with 7 percent from high-tension respondents. This also shows up in the highest giving category, where nearly one high-tension member out of five gave $5,000 or more in 2006, compared with 4 percent of those in lower-tension churches.

OUTREACH

Given the high levels of morale and commitment in the high-tension churches, it seems likely that they will be more active and effective at outreach. This is clearly the case:

	High tension	Low tension
TABLE 15		
Tension and Witnessing		
Witnessed to *friends* in the past month	64%	34%
Witnessed to *strangers* in the past month	43%	19%

High-tension respondents are about twice as likely to tell friends about their faith—and these are the people who can more easily be brought into membership in their churches. But high-tension respondents are also far more active in witnessing to strangers. And, as was seen in the previous chapter, willingness of members to tell others about their religion translates into rapid growth rates for high-tension denominations.

CONCLUSION

The findings in this chapter can be summed up in a sentence: strict churches are strong because groups that ask more from their members get more from them, which provides them with the resources to provide a more satisfying religious "product."

Contributor: Christopher Bader

The "Scattered" Church
Traditional Congregations Are Not Going Away

Among the new buzz words about American religious life are the "scattered" and the "gathered" church. These terms arise from two very contradictory claims, both involving perceived failures of the conventional churches.

On the one hand are claims that the church is becoming too scattered: many nondenominational religious groups have arisen that maintain no connections with organized churches, such as groups meeting regularly to hold prayer breakfasts and independent Bible-study groups made up of people who otherwise shun participation in religious activities or church congregations. This form of the scattered church is often read not only as a symptom of the demise of denominationalism but also as a sign that augurs the decline of organized religion in general.

On the other hand, many critics condemn the churches for not being scattered enough. They accuse American congregations of being too gathered (or closed) and therefore of failing to reach out and give active witness in the world. That is, the virtue of the gathered church is not to be found in its capacity to create a community of devotion but primarily in the extent to which it supports ministries in nontraditional, external settings.

Of course, both complaints could be true—that there are many scattered groups of Christians fully separated from the churches, and that most congregations promote such scattering by being far too gathered. Both complaints could also be false. Unfortunately, as so often happens, these claims about the scattered and gathered church have inspired a good deal of passion, but they are based on very little evidence. Consequently, proper items were included in the 2007 Baylor Survey to shed light on these issues.

IS THE CHURCH TOO SCATTERED?

Recently, D. Michael Lindsay lamented that many of the prominent people he interviewed as part of his study of the evangelical elite frequently attend such things as prayer breakfasts, but "can't be found in the pews on Sunday."[1] As a case in point, he notes that although President Bush does attend chapel services when he is at Camp David, unlike presidents Carter and Clinton he rarely attends a church in Washington, D.C. Lindsay ignored the possibility that President Bush wishes to avoid imposing the disruption that is entailed by presidential attendance on a congregation, especially given opposition to the war in Iraq. Nor did Lindsay seem to recognize that many of his other prominent evangelical interviewees may avoid *all* activities not limited to a small circle of persons of similar status. Perhaps they are comfortable at a prayer breakfast with other executives, for example, but avoid public gatherings at such places as churches, movie theaters, and even airports, and only attend sporting events if they have private suites.

Be that as it may, Robert Wuthnow has made far broader claims about the extent of the scattered church and what it means.[2] He sees the strength of the gathered denominations being drained away and scattered into the hundreds of these special-purpose groups, making it impossible to sustain a diverse congregation in the face of the intense loyalty generated by special-purpose religious groups, such as those consisting only of motorcyclists, feminists, divorcées, gays, rock fans, peace activists, and the like. Wuthnow stresses how this will fragment religion; it might also be suggested that such developments trivialize it as well.

Three items were asked to measure participation in the scattered church.

"How often did you participate in the following religious activities in the last month?"

—A community prayer group not affiliated with/sponsored by a congregation:

Not at all	86%
1–2 times	10%
3–4 times	2%
5 or more	2%
	100%

—A community Bible study not affiliated with/sponsored by a congregation:

Not at all	91%
1–2 times	6%
3–4 times	2%
5 or more	1%
	100%

—Faith-based programs not affiliated with/sponsored by a congregation:

Not at all	88%
1–2 times	8%
3–4 times	2%
5 or more	2%
	100%

These three questions provide an important finding—the scattered church appears to be quite large. Fourteen percent of American adults—or about 31 million people—take part in a community prayer group, 9 percent in a Bible-study group, and 12 percent in faith-based programs not affiliated with or sponsored by a congregation. The key question is, are these "scattered" activities substituted for participation in the gathered church?

Absolutely not. The data demonstrate just the opposite. Of the 168 respondents in the 2007 Baylor Survey who take part in a prayer group, only seven of them fit Lindsay's description by attending church once or twice a year or less. Eighty percent are very frequent attenders—24 percent attend several times a week. Participation in a prayer group augments and expands their congregational worship; it does not weaken or replace it. One supposes that nondenominational prayer groups actually strengthen the gathered church.

The same is true for those who take part in Bible-study groups. Only 5 percent of those who attend these groups attend church only once or twice a year or less; 80 percent attend at least two or three times a month; 25 percent attend more often than once a week. These statistics are repeated for participation in faith-based activities.

Finally, those who are active in the scattered church are also socially very active in their congregations: 76 percent of those who take part in noncongregational prayer groups report that they attended a social gathering in their churches in the past month. The claim that the churches are scattering and thereby suffering a loss of commitment is simply false.

In addition:

• *Denomination*: There are no meaningful patterns across the denominations, people from the liberal denominations being about as likely as those from the more conservative groups to participate in the scattered church.

• *Education*: Education has no effects, not even on participation in Bible-study groups.

• *Gender*: There are no gender differences.

• *Race*: There are substantial racial differences, African Americans being about twice as likely as whites to take part in scattered church activities.

• *Region*: People living in the South are the most likely to take part in the scattered church; those in the West are the least likely to do so—these differences partly reflect differences in racial composition.

IS THE CHURCH TOO GATHERED?

Many pastors and church leaders have said amen to the indictment of American churches so recently leveled by the Baptist leader Edward H. Hammett.[3] Acknowledging that the churches must be gathered in order to have the capacity to serve, Hammett nonetheless asserts that the churches are failing in their fundamental gospel mission because they are too gathered to reach out beyond their congregational boundaries. According to Hammett, "we keep getting stuck in an inward focus, thinking about the life of the institution, trying to build it up for itself. We keep losing sight of the fact that its task is not to build itself up, but to enhance the flow of the people of God into the world."[4]

This is, of course, a very old criticism that probably was first heard in the days of the apostles. But is it true? The primary issue is whether or not congregations tend to be open or closed social networks and whether this influences their capacity for outreach. To assess how open or closed the churches are respondents were asked:

"How many of your friends attend your place of worship?"

None	19%
A few	49%
About half	14%
Most	16%
All	2%
	100%

First of all, two-thirds of those Americans who attend a place of worship do not belong to a gathered church in that they have none or only a few of their friends in their congregations, and only 18 percent have most or all of their friends in their congregations. A second aspect of the gathered church has to do with volunteer efforts within one's congregation. Respondents were asked:

"About how many hours per month do you volunteer for your place of worship?"

None	71%
1–2 hours	14%
3–4 hours	8%
5–10 hours	4%
11 or more	3%
	100%

More than one American in four does some volunteer service every month for his or her place of worship—keep in mind that this statistic includes the unchurched and the irreligious. Perhaps surprisingly, men and women are equally likely to be volunteers, and there is no difference in the number of hours they put in. However, volunteering is extremely correlated with having friends in one's congregation: 20 percent of those having no friends in their congregation volunteer, while 60 percent with half or more of their friends in their congregation do so. This makes perfect sense. How do people become volunteers? Not usually in response to billboards or mail solicitations but because someone they know invites them to do so. This is far more likely to happen in congregations integrated by friendship ties than in congregations that are as impersonal as movie audiences.

The issue is, of course, what difference does it make? Do these aspects of the gathered church reflect congregations turned inward and lacking outreach?

One of Hammett's major concerns about the lack of outreach by the gathered church has to do with its alleged failure to sustain a ministry to the world. To address this concern, the following item was included in the 2007 Baylor Survey:

"How often did you participate in the following religious or faith-based activities in the last month?

—*Witnessing/sharing your faith with strangers*

Not at all	70%
1–2 times	21%
3–4 times	5%
5 or more	4%
	100%

Thirty percent of all Americans have witnessed in the past month. But according to Hammett, those immersed in gathered churches are unlikely to be among that 30 percent—that in churches that constitute friendship networks, members are content to sustain a closed Christian community.[5] That may sound plausible, but the data support the opposite conclusion.

TABLE 16

Congregational Friendships and Witnessing

"How many of your friends attend your place of worship?"

	None	Some	Half or more
Percent who witnessed	15%	29%	44%

As Table 16 shows, it is members of the gathered church who most often witness to strangers. There is also another major aspect of outreach: volunteering for community service.

"About how many hours per month do you volunteer for the community through your place of worship?"

None	65%
1–2 hours	18%
3–4 hours	9%
5–10 hours	4%
11 or more	4%
	100%

A third of all Americans do monthly volunteer services in their communities through programs sustained by their places of worship.

TABLE 17

Congregational Friendships and Volunteering

"How many of your friends attend your place of worship?"

	None	Some	Half or more
Percent who volunteered	14%	31%	52%

Keep in mind that all of those included in this table have a place of worship. Clearly, belonging to a congregation that consists largely of close friendship clusters does not turn members inward. Here, too, it is members of the most gathered churches who are the ones most likely to do volunteer work in their communities.

These findings will confirm what many pastors and lay leaders have observed and believed all along—scattered activities outside the gathered church not only may benefit those receiving the outreach, but will usually encourage and strengthen the commitment of those providing the outreach. The scattered and gathered churches strengthen each other, a classic win-win proposition.

CONCLUSION

The most persistent feature about critiques of the American churches is that they are failing, that catastrophe looms: denominationalism is doomed. Young people are deserting in droves. Attendance is in rapid decline and so is church membership. The churches are too scattered. The churches are too gathered.

But the appropriate data demonstrate that each of these claims is false. Instead, each is a figment of the overactive imaginations of those who fear these charges may be true and, perhaps, of some who desperately hope that they are.

MEGACHURCHES
Supersizing the Faith

The rise of Protestant megachurches has caused a great deal of comment and criticism. Some media find them appalling examples of a religious "Disneyland" mentality wherein people flock to be part of an anonymous crowd of spectators rather than worshipers. It is widely believed that to be really close to God, one should worship in a small, intimate congregation, surrounded by fellow worshipers who have a proper awareness that faith must recognize sin, not just happy returns. Many claim that the megachurches draw huge crowds because, as the distinguished *Newsweek* religion writer Kenneth Woodward put it, they "tend to be a guilt-free, sin-free environment.... These places are a bit too bubbly."[1] Even Leith Anderson, the pastor of a megachurch in Minnesota, has charged that most other megachurches offer sermons "about practical biblical tips for successful living, and go light on doctrine and sin."[2] This, presumably, stands in contrast to the greater authenticity, commitment, and intimacy of small congregations.

Charges like these have often been denied, but there has been a lack of hard evidence. So the 2007 Baylor Survey asked people "On average, how many people attend services at your place of worship?" Looking only at Protestants, this question allows the creation of two kinds of congregations: the small congregation having a usual attendance of less than 100, and the megachurch having attendance greater than 1,000. By comparing these two types of congregations on a multitude of matters, it was possible to see if the small congregation does in fact provide its members with a superior religious experience. (No interpretation would be changed if the congregations of sizes in between these were shown in the tables.)

We begin with the charge that the megachurches sustain an easy, comfortable faith and soft-pedal sin and punishment. As Woodward put it, "Sin really has disappeared from the pulpit. It's too much of a downer, I'm afraid."[3]

TABLE 18
On the "Bright Side"

	Megachurches	Small congregations
Heaven "absolutely" exists	92%	79%
Very, or quite, certain you will get into heaven	85%	53%
The Rapture[4] will "absolutely" take place	82%	49%
Agree: "God rewards the faithful with major successes"	57%	46%

Clearly, members of megachurches are more likely than those in small congregations to accept the "bright side" of faith—to believe they are going to heaven and are apt to receive worldly rewards.

But, contrary to their critics, members of the megachurches are not sitting in comfortable pews, basking in a sunny religion that preaches only the bright side of faith. Yes, they are more confident of God's rewards than are those in the small churches, but they also are more convinced of the reality of evil, as we see in Table 19.

	Megachurches	Small congregations
TABLE 19 *On the "Dark Side"*		
Hell "absolutely" exists	90%	69%
Devil/Satan "absolutely" exists	83%	66%
Agree that God "is angered by human sin"	72%	67%

There also are many critics who think the megachurches thrive on people who enjoy dramatic Sunday service with fine music but don't wish to become very "religious" on a day-to-day basis—that the megachurch appeal is a mile wide and an inch deep.

	Megachurches	Small congregations
TABLE 20 *Personal Commitment*		
Attend services weekly or more often	46%	39%
Tithe	46%	36%
Pray at least once a day or more often	60%	61%
Read the Bible daily	33%	32%
Attend a Bible-study group	52%	43%

But it is not true. Those who belong to megachurches display as high a level of personal commitment as do those who attend small congregations.

TABLE 21
Religious and Mystical Experiences

	Megachurches	Small congregations
Index of Religious and Mystical Experience:		
High	67%	39%
Medium	15%	18%
Low	15%	19%
None	3%	24%
	100%	100%

Moreover, members of megachurches are far more given to having religious and mystical experiences—half say they have "heard the voice of God speaking to me." (See chapter 6 for an explanation of the Index of Religious and Mystical Experience.)

But what about the lack of intimacy that supposedly results from worshiping with so many people?

TABLE 22
Intimacy

	Megachurches	Small congregations
Half or more of their friends attend their congregations	41%	25%
Have *no* friends in their congregations	12%	22%

So much for the nostalgic image of the small congregation as a community of intimates. In the sense of having friends in the congregation, the megachurch is the more intimate community. One reason for this is evident when outreach is examined.

	Megachurches	Small congregations
TABLE 23 *Outreach*		
In the past month did you: Witness/share your faith with friends	83%	52%
Witness/share your faith with strangers	53%	35%

A major reason that so many people in the megachurches have so many friends in their congregation is because they *brought* them into the group—83 percent have witnessed to their friends in the past month (35 percent have done so three times or more). Megachurch members also greatly outdo members of the small churches by witnessing to strangers. Contrary to the widespread conviction among their critics that the megachurches grow mainly through their ability to gain publicity, their growth appears instead mainly to be the result of their members' outreach efforts.

Of course, some critics of the megachurches attack them precisely because they are communities. The sociologist Wade Clark Roof has claimed that the megachurch is "the religious version of the gated community. . . . It's an attempt to create a world where you're dealing with like-minded people. . . . You lose the dialogue with the larger culture." And a prominent church historian at Wake Forest University disdained megachurches for "Christian cocooning."[5] Let's see about that.

TABLE 24
Volunteerism

	Megachurches	Small congregations
I do volunteer work: for the community, not through my place of worship	40%	31%
for the community, through my place of worship	41%	34%
During the past month participated in faith-based programs not affiliated or sponsored by a congregation (e.g., prison ministry, homeless shelter, etc.)	18%	9%

Another myth shattered. Members of megachurches are remarkably active in volunteer work, as much or more so than those in the tiny churches.

Finally, compared with megachurches, small congregations are significantly older—almost half of their members are over 50. This is consistent with the assumption that small congregations often are dying congregations, which is supported by the fact that they are very apt to be affiliated with a liberal denomination that has long been shrinking (see chapter 2).

TABLE 25
Demographics

	Megachurches	Small congregations
Age of church members:		
70 and over	6%	12%
50–59	26%	35%
Church affiliation with liberal Protestant denominations	21%	47%

CONCLUSION

It is all well and good to suppose that worship would be more satisfying in a small church with only a few in the pews, and one has a perfect right to suppose that much is lost when one worships with thousands. Indeed, among the things that are lost is the uninspired sound of hymns sung by a few dozen reluctant voices, as compared to the "joyful noise" of thousands of voices, of large and talented choirs, and even the strains from professional orchestras that provide the music in the leading megachurches. Also lost is the perception that the band of faithful is old, small, and getting smaller. Finally, what is lost is the reluctance to spread the Good Tidings to others.

PART II

BELIEFS AND PRACTICES

RELIGIOUS EXPERIENCES
God Told Me to Go to Church

*A*merican Piety pioneered the surveying of religious and mystical experiences. Having defined religious experiences as involving *some sense of contact with a supernatural being or consciousness*, the researchers prepared a battery of items asking about events involving various kinds of visions, voices, and miracles. Unfortunately, the authors let themselves be talked out of including most of these items when several of their theological consultants, Martin E. Marty and David Noel Freedman among them, objected, saying the questions postulated behavior so extreme and bizarre that to include them would offend almost all respondents.

So out went nearly all the items, and the only ones that remained were quite vague. One asked whether respondents had ever had the "feeling that you were somehow in the presence of God," and another asked whether they ever had "a sense of being saved in Christ." The theologians were not very happy to have even these bland questions included in the study. But when 73 percent of the Protestant church members and 66 percent of the Roman Catholics said they had felt themselves in the presence of God, and 60 percent of the Protestants and 48 percent of the Catholics said they had been saved in Christ, it was obvious that the theologians were out of touch with the people in the pews. The more "extreme" questions should have been asked.

In the years that followed, a bit of attention was paid to religious experiences. Unfortunately, the questions were either as vague and as widely accepted as those in the original *American Piety* questionnaire—for example, Gallup found that 82 percent of Americans agreed that "I am sometimes very conscious of the presence of God"—or the questions dealt with things better described as paranormal experiences, such as the battery of questions included for many years in the General Social Surveys.[1] Placed amidst items asking about experiencing déjà vu or having foreknowledge of distant events, only one item could be interpreted as involving a religious experience, and even it had New Age overtones: "How often have you felt as though you were very close to a powerful, spiritual force that seemed to lift you out of yourself?" Thirty-seven percent of Americans said they had undergone such an experience. Even so, the reluctance to address serious kinds of religious and mystical experiences persisted.

The Baylor Surveys included the kinds of questions that should have been included in the *American Piety* study forty years ago. Respondents were asked:

"Please indicate whether or not you have ever had any of the following experiences":

"I heard the voice of God speaking to me."

                          Yes   20%

So much for claims made by theologians before the *American Piety* surveys went into the field that not even 0.1 percent of Americans have had such an experience and that most of them would be living in mental hospitals. Much to the contrary, one American in five has heard God speaking to her or him.

"I felt called by God to do something."

                          Yes   44%

Here, too, a very large number of Americans seem to feel God working in their lives.

"I was protected from harm by a guardian angel."

Yes   55%

What an extraordinary finding. Many will no doubt try to explain this away by claiming that people did not mean this literally—that this is merely a figure of speech by which people acknowledge a lucky break. But it seems much more likely that people actually meant what the item says, given that 61 percent believe "absolutely" that angels exist and another 21 percent of American adults think they "probably" exist. No wonder that television series such as *Touched by an Angel*, have been so popular.

"I witnessed a miraculous, physical healing."

Yes   23%

No metaphors here. Twenty-three percent of Americans believe they have witnessed a miraculous healing. It should be pointed out that there is a huge and rapidly growing literature on the strong positive effects of religion on physical and mental health—a research enterprise conducted by highly respected medical scientists. Even so, probably no one anticipated this:

"I received a miraculous, physical healing."

Yes   16%

How remarkable. Not surprisingly, since one needs to be ill before one could be healed, there is a modest but significant age effect: 12 percent of those under 30 say they have been miraculously healed, compared with 22 percent of those over 70. Women (18%) are a bit more likely than men (13%) to say they have been healed.

Finally:

"I spoke or prayed in tongues."

Yes   8%

This item does not reflect a general mystical phenomenon but is intrinsic to Pentecostal forms of worship and pretty much limited to participants in Pentecostal churches—it is not very highly correlated with the other items.

However, the first five items are highly intercorrelated, and therefore it was appropriate to use them to create a simple additive index of religious experiences. Scoring one point for each yes answer, the resulting index ranged from zero to five. However, since only 5 percent of the population scored five, the index was collapsed as shown:

(3–5)	High	27%
(2)	Medium	18%
(1)	Low	21%
(0)	None	34%

Note that only 34 percent of Americans answered no to all five questions.

TABLE 26
Denomination and Index of Religious & Mystical Experiences

	Percent High	Percent Medium	Combined
Unitarian	0%	20%	20%
United Church of Christ	10%	10%	20%
Presbyterian	16%	19%	35%
Lutheran	17%	18%	35%
Episcopalian	24%	13%	37%
Methodist	24%	25%	49%
All Liberal Protestants	20%	20%	40%
Baptist	37%	22%	59%
Pentecostal	70%	18%	88%
Assemblies of God	81%	5%	86%
All Conservative Protestants	44%	20%	64%
Roman Catholic	20%	20%	40%
Latter-day Saints (Mormon)	53%	33%	86%
Jewish	7%	2%	9%

Clearly denomination matters—conservative Protestants are more likely than liberal Protestants, Catholics, or Jews to report religious and mystical experiences. However, it is equally apparent that religious experiences are not limited to conservative Protestants but occur with considerable frequency in nearly all religious groups—even 20 percent of Unitarians reported two or more such experiences.

As for other factors that might influence the frequency of religious experiences:

- *Gender*: Women (50 percent reported two or more experiences) were more apt to have them than men (38%).

- *Race*: African Americans (68%) scored higher than whites (43%).

- *Education*: Education had no significant effect: people who attended graduate school (41%) were as likely to report religious experiences as were those who did not attend college (43%).

- *Age*: Nor did age matter: 42 percent of those under thirty reported two or more religious experiences and so did the same percentage of those over seventy.

- *Region*: Regional variations were very small and merely reflected differences in racial composition.

- *Politics*: Republicans (55%) were more likely than Democrats (38%) to have religious and mystical experiences, and the differences were even greater when examined among whites only.

CONCLUSION

Religious and mystical experiences are the overlooked aspect of our national religious life—neglected by researchers and ignored or even denied by leading theologians and seminary professors. Yet, these experiences are so intrinsic to American religion that two out of every three respondents reported having at least one of those experiences asked about in the 2007 Baylor Survey, and 45 percent report having had two or more.

While these findings will surprise most contemporary observers of religion (and no doubt will upset many of them as well), the findings would not have surprised any of the very first social scientists to study religious behavior. More than a century ago, such important figures as William James,[2] Edwin Diller Starbuck,[3] and Evelyn Underhill[4] placed religious and mystical experiences at the center of their writing and research. It is time to do so again.

GENDER
Women Believe More, Pray More

Historians agree that women greatly outnumbered men among the converts to early Christianity.[1] The great German scholar Adolf von Harnack wrote that the ancient sources "simply swarm with tales of how women of all ranks were converted in Rome and in the provinces."[2] This was not peculiar to the early Christian church. Greek and Roman writers routinely "portrayed women as particularly liable to succumb to the charms of [new religions]."[3] Thus, for example, as the cult of Isis spread west from Egypt, it attracted mainly a female following, as did the cult of Dionysus.[4]

The overrepresentation of women in religious groups and movements is not limited to classic times. Even today, women outnumber men in all of the organized denominations. Nor is this simply because women outlive men. It is true even among young people. And it is not merely a matter of belonging to churches—by any measure, women are more religious than men.

Women (69%) are more likely than men (57%) to believe in God without doubts or reservations, and men are twice as likely as women to be atheists. Also women (77%) are more likely than men (68%) to believe that Jesus is the Son of God. See the following tables.

TABLE 27
Gender and Religious Beliefs

Which one statement comes closest to your personal beliefs about God?

	Females	Males	Total sample
I have *no doubts* that God exists	69%	57%	63%
I believe in God, but with *some doubts*	10%	14%	12%
I *sometimes believe* in God	2%	2%	2%
I believe in a *higher power* or cosmic force	12%	12%	12%
I don't know, and there is no way to find out	4%	8%	6%
I am an atheist	2%	6%	4%
I have no opinion	1%	1%	1%
	100%	100%	100%

Which one statement comes closest to your personal beliefs about Jesus?

	Females	Males	Total sample
Jesus is the Son of God	77%	68%	73%
Jesus was one of many messengers or prophets of God	10%	11%	11%

Jesus was an extraordinary person, but he was not the Son of God	5%	10%	7%
Jesus probably existed, but he was not special	2%	4%	3%
Jesus is a fictional character	1%	2%	1%
I have no opinion	5%	5%	5%
	100%	100%	100%

In your opinion, does each of the following exist?

	Females	Males	Total sample
The Devil/Satan			
Absolutely	59%	48%	54%
Probably	19%	20%	20%
Hell			
Absolutely	58%	47%	53%
Probably	20%	20%	20%
Demons			
Absolutely	50%	40%	45%
Probably	23%	21%	22%
Heaven			
Absolutely	68%	56%	62%
Probably	19%	20%	20%
Angels			
Absolutely	68%	52%	61%
Probably	20%	22%	21%

Belief runs high on all of these items, but in every case women are substantially more likely than men to accept them.

TABLE 28

Gender and Religious Behavior

	Females	Males	Total Sample
Attends church weekly	40%	31%	36%
Prays at least once a day	57%	40%	49%
Reads the Bible weekly	32%	24%	28%
High on Index of Religious and Mystical Experience	31%	22%	27%

Here too women excel. Forty percent of women attend church weekly compared with 31 percent of men. Fifty-seven percent of women pray at least once a day, compared with 40 percent of men. And a third of women read the Bible weekly or more often, while only 24 percent of men do likewise. Finally, women are more likely (31%) to score high on the Index of Religious and Mystical Experience than are men (22%).

TABLE 29

Gender and Religiousness

How religious do you consider yourself?

	Females	Males	Total sample
Very religious	37%	25%	31%
Somewhat religious	41%	44%	42%
Not too religious	13%	16%	15%
Not at all religious	8%	14%	11%
I don't know	1%	1%	1%
	100%	100%	100%

If a survey could ask only one item about an individual's religiousness, the best choice is to ask them directly, as in Table 29. People understand such a question and seem very willing to assess themselves—this question predicts other measures such as frequency of church attendance and prayer and certainty of religious beliefs remarkably well.

These gender differences are not found only in America. A similar question ("I am a religious person" agree/disagree) has been asked in fifty-five other nations. In each nation, women were considerably more likely than men to agree that they were religious persons, usually by very wide margins. This also held in non-Christian societies, including Japan, China, South Korea, and India. Even in Islamic nations, where women often are excluded from mosques or required to sit out of sight in balconies, women are more likely to be religious than are men.[5] So far as can be determined, the gender difference in religiousness is universal.

For a long time it was assumed that these differences simply reflect differences in the socialization of men and women—that girls are raised with higher expectations that they will be religious than are boys. But efforts to demonstrate that socialization is the cause have been remarkably unsuccessful. For example, several studies found that career women are as religious as are homemakers, and both differ considerably from men. Another approach suggested that if the gender differences in religiousness result from differences in sex-role socialization, then gender differences in religiousness should be smaller in the United States today than they were decades ago. But when data for the early 1970s were compared with the most recent data, the gender differences were precisely the same. Another approach supposed that if the gender differences are rooted in traditional sex roles, then men and women who reject traditional beliefs about sex roles should be more alike in terms of their religiousness. But it is not so. Then it was suggested that gender differences in religiousness will be greater in societies where more traditional sex roles prevail and women's primary roles tend to be limited to home and family than in societies where there is far greater gender equality. Again, the data was contrary—if anything, gender differences in religiousness are even greater in the *less* traditional societies.

At that point, the late Alan Miller, an American professor at a Japanese university, noted that the only similarly "universal" gender difference is that men greatly surpass women in the commission of crimes and reckless behaviors (speeding, smoking, not fastening seat belts, etc.). In a brilliant article Miller reasoned that irreligiousness resembles criminal and other risky behaviors in that many religions postulate serious consequences for irreligiousness, and hence just as a burglar risks jail, an atheist risks hell. So, just as some men are more willing than most women to risk jail by gambling that they won't get caught for a crime, they also are more willing to be irreligious and gamble that there is no hell. Although working with less than ideal data, Miller found that men and women with similar scores on a measure of risk-taking were similar in their religiousness.[6] A subsequent study found that gender differences are larger in religions that hold that there are serious punishments in store for the irreligious and smaller in religions, such as Buddhism, that do not have such doctrines.[7]

The 2007 Baylor Religion Survey included an item (see below) that permits a very rough test of the risk-taking explanation of the gender differences in religiousness.

Table 30 shows there is a quite significant gender difference in responses to the risk-taking question: men are more than twice as likely as women to agree strongly that they like doing things for a thrill, and the majority of men (52%), compared with only a third (35%) of women, agree to any degree. If a male affinity for risky behavior does account for the gender differences in religion, then the differences ought to vanish when the religiousness of men and women who strongly agreed with this question about thrills are compared.

TABLE 30
Gender and Risk

"I like doing things for a thrill"

	Females	Males	Total sample
Strongly agree	4%	10%	7%
Agree	31%	42%	36%
Disagree	44%	38%	41%
Strongly disagree	15%	6%	11%
Undecided	6%	4%	5%
	100%	100%	100%

TABLE 31
Gender, Religiousness, and Risk

[Only those who absolutely agreed they like to do things for a thrill]
"How religious do you consider yourself?"

	Females	Males	Total sample
Very religious	27%	30%	29%
Somewhat religious	38%	35%	36%
Total	*65%*	*65%*	*65%*
Attend church weekly	30%	29%	29%
"I have no doubts that God exists"	67%	63%	65%
High on Index of Religious and Mystical Experiences	37%	36%	36%

Among the risk takers there are no significant gender differences. Once again, Miller's explanation is confirmed.

CONCLUSION

Of course, the question persists: why do men and women differ in their propensity for risky behavior? A case can be made for a genetic difference, that group survival is enhanced by having males with a genetic willingness to take chances and do risky things such as fighting. A case also can be made that group survival is enhanced by raising males in ways that make them risk takers. This is an extraordinarily difficult matter to sort out. Meanwhile, in every society we know about, women were, or are, more religious than men.

HEAVEN
We Are All Going

Although the Gallup poll found in 1957 that 74 percent of Americans said they believed in life after death (and another 13 percent said they were undecided),[1] by the time of the survey conducted for *American Piety* in 1964, it was widely believed that most Americans didn't really mean it. Not only were many liberal theologians convinced that heaven was merely a metaphor, but they were equally sure that's how most Americans viewed the matter and that only backward fundamentalists still believed in a literal life beyond death. It came as something of a surprise to many when the national survey conducted in 1964 found that 47 percent of Americans said they were "absolutely sure" there was life after death and another 32 percent were "pretty sure," making a combined total of 79 percent.

Subsequently, beginning in 1973, the General Social Surveys frequently asked "Do you believe there is a life after death?" Year after year, through 2002, about 70 percent of Americans answered "yes" and another 8 or 9 percent said they were "undecided."

The 2005 Baylor Survey shifted from asking about belief in a life after death to asking about belief in heaven. Sixty-seven percent said they were "absolutely sure" heaven exists, and 17 percent thought it "probably" does, for a total of 84 percent. Quite similar percentages gave these responses when the question was repeated in the 2007 Baylor Survey (see Table 32).

Not surprisingly, the certainty of a person's belief in heaven is related to religious affiliation, although the overwhelming majority in all Christian groups are at least pretty sure heaven exists. The statistic for Jews is based on rather few cases. However, it is consistent with the findings based on the combined General Social Surveys (yielding a total of 611 Jews) that 33 percent of Jews believe in life after death—the small difference between the two percentages could easily have been due to the reluctance of some Jews to accept the term "heaven."

TABLE 32
Religious Affiliation and Belief in Heaven

	Absolutely sure	Pretty sure
Conservative Protestants	89%	7%
Liberal Protestants	60%	25%
Roman Catholics	62%	28%
Jews	0%	23%
All Americans	63%	19%

In addition to denomination, other factors influence belief in heaven, too:

• *Gender*: Women (68%) are more likely than men (56%) to be absolutely sure there is a heaven.

• *Race*: African Americans (86%) are more apt to be certain than are whites (60%).

• *Education*: Persons who did not enter college (70%) are more likely to be absolutely sure than are those who attended graduate school (43%).

• *Age*: Age has no effect.

- *Region*: Certainty that Heaven exists is highest in the South (76%) and lowest in the East (50%).
- *Politics*: Republicans (77%) are more likely to be absolutely sure there is a heaven than are Democrats (54%).

Unlike previous surveys, the 2007 Baylor Survey asked additional questions about heaven. One of them:

"How certain are you that you will get to heaven?"

Very certain	30%
Quite certain	16%
Somewhat certain	20%
Not very certain	4%
Not at all certain	3%
I don't know	16%
I don't believe in heaven	11%
	100%

Overall, 46 percent of Americans are at least "quite certain" they will go to heaven, and another 20 percent are "somewhat certain."

TABLE 33
Religious Affiliation and Going to Heaven

	Very or quite certain
Conservative Protestants	67%
Liberal Protestants	46%
Roman Catholics	36%
Jews	7%
All Americans	46%

Denomination matters here, too, with conservative Protestants tending to be rather more certain that they are heaven-bound than are members of other denominations.

• *Gender*: Women (51%) are more apt than men (39%) to be very or quite certain they are going to heaven.

• *Race*: African Americans (55%) are more certain than are whites (45%).

• *Age*: Age doesn't matter.

• *Region*: Southerners (54%) are more likely than people in other regions to be confident that they are saved, while people in the East and the West (39%) are least certain.

• *Education*: Education makes very little difference.

• *Politics*: Republicans (61%) are more certain than are Democrats (34%).

In addition, respondents were asked about who will get into heaven.

TABLE 34
Who and How Many Will Get into Heaven?

"If you believe in heaven, how many of the following people do you think will get into heaven?"

	Half or more	A few	None	No opinion	
Average Americans	54%	16%	1%	29%	100%
Christians	72%	6%	1%	21%	100%
Jews	46%	11%	6%	37%	100%
Buddhists	37%	8%	16%	39%	100%
Muslims	34%	11%	16%	39%	100%
Nonreligious people	29%	13%	21%	37%	100%

The primary finding here is that few Americans think heaven is very exclusive. Only 29 percent think that even the irreligious are prevented from entering. Granted, large numbers admit to having no opinion as to who will or won't be admitted, but in this instance it would seem that no opinion is a very meaningful response. Unlike earlier generations of Americans, most of whom held strong views that the "Pearly Gates" were very narrow (in 1964, 52 percent said that a person who did not accept Jesus could not be saved),[2] few now expect heaven to be restricted to Christians.

The Baylor Survey also asked people whether or not Hell exists. Fifty-three percent responded "Absolutely," another 20 percent selected "Probably," 16 percent answered "Probably not," and 11 percent checked "Absolutely not." That 73 percent think hell exists is a bit lower than the 82 percent who believe in heaven, but it is much higher than most commentators on American religion seem to have assumed. Alan F. Segal of Columbia University has claimed that belief in hell is now limited to "the Evangelical and Fundamentalist communities."[3] But that's obviously not so.

TABLE 35
Religious Affiliation and Belief in Hell

	Absolutely or probably exists
Conservative Protestants	92%
Liberal Protestants	69%
Roman Catholics	79%
Jews	3%
All Americans	73%

American Christians of all denominations overwhelmingly believe hell exists.

Furthermore:

• *Gender*: Women (78%) are more likely than men (67%) to believe in hell.

• *Race*: African Americans (92%) are more likely than whites (71%) to believe in hell.

• *Region*: Midwesterners (80%) and Southerners (81%) are more likely to believe in hell than are Easterners (64%) and Westerners (63%).

• *Education*: People who did not attend college (79%) are more likely to believe than are those who attended graduate school (54%).

• *Age*: People of all ages are equally likely to believe in hell.

• *Politics*: Republicans (86%) are more likely than Democrats (65%) to believe in hell.

Conclusion

Americans overwhelmingly believe in an afterlife, in heaven, and equally in hell. Not only that, most of them expect to go to heaven. The survey did not ask about going to hell—maybe next time.

GOD

Love, Anger, and Commitment

I n 1944 the Gallup poll asked a national sample of Americans, "Do you, personally, believe in God?" and 96 percent said "yes." Through the decades that same question has been asked many times, and the results are always the same: just about everyone believes in God. What that means, of course, is that to know that Americans believe in God tells us almost nothing about them except that they are not atheists. It is nearly useless to continue to ask people if they believe in God without finding out what they mean by "God."

Some think of God as an angry man in the sky who expresses his displeasure through disasters and misfortune. To others, God is an expression of unending love and compassion who provides strength, inspiration, and forgiveness. Still others imagine a God that is more of a cosmic force than a personality—a force of great power but removed from direct involvement in world affairs. Clearly, an individual who views God as an abstract, cosmic force and an individual who views God as a white-bearded man sitting in the clouds cannot be said to believe in the same God. We would expect the effect of God on each of these individuals to be very different.

The 2007 Baylor Survey asked a detailed battery of items regarding how people perceive God's nature and character.

Several underlying images of God emerged, and two of these provide the focus of this chapter. The first perceives God as being *benevolent* and deeply *engaged* in human affairs. The second image sees God as *judgmental* and *severe*.

Based on your personal understanding, what do you think God is like?

[Items depicting God as benevolent and engaged]

	Strongly agree	Agree
1. Concerned with the well-being of the world	50%	28%
2. Concerned with my personal well-being	50%	26%
3. Directly involved in worldly affairs	26%	26%
4. Directly involved in my affairs	32%	28%

[Items depicting God as judgmental and severe]

1. Angered by human sin	31%	26%
2. Angered by my sins	26%	27%

How well do you feel that each of the following words describe God in your opinion?

[Words depicting God as benevolent and engaged]

Distant*	6%	11%
Ever-present	71%	14%

[Words depicting God as judgmental and severe]

Critical	12%	14%
Punishing	19%	19%

Severe	13%	13%
Wrathful	14%	16%

* Scored in reverse as *not* distant in the Engaged God Index.

Examining the items it seems apparent that these two very distinct images of God reflect differences sometimes attributed to God as depicted in the Old and New Testaments—the rumbling God of Mount Sinai versus the forgiving Father of Jesus. It also is apparent that Americans tend to prefer the more benevolent and engaged God to the severe God of judgment.

These two sets of items were scored to create an Index of an Engaged God and an Index of a Judging God. These indexes permit investigation of a key question: which image of God motivates greater religious commitment? That is, are people more religious because of fear or gratitude? Many informed observers would predict that fear trumps gratitude. Table 36 uses a very simple measure called correlation. A correlation measures the strength of the relationship between two factors, such as between the frequency of church attendance and gender. If there were no difference between men and women in their frequency of church attendance, the correlation would be 0.00, which means the relationship is nonexistent. If all women attended weekly and no men ever go to church, the correlation would be 1.00, which means the relationship between the two is perfect. Of course, most correlations fall far short of perfect, so the focus is on which ones are higher than others. In the application shown in Table 36, the correlations compare the strength of the relationship between each index of God's nature and a series of measures of religiousness to see if they differ.

TABLE 36

Images of God and Religious Commitment

	Index of engaged God	Index of judging God
Frequency of prayer	.647	.185
Church attendance	.588	.211
Index of Religious Experiences	.646	.176
Frequency of Bible reading	.593	.243
Identification as a religious person	.675	.275
Witnessing to strangers	.445	.171

It isn't even close. Conceiving of God as benevolent and engaged is very highly correlated with a variety of aspects of commitment, from prayer to regarding oneself as a religious person. In contrast, seeing God as judgmental is only very weakly related to these aspects of commitment. In fact, when a statistical technique known as regression analysis is used to extract the independent effects of each index, it turns out that seeing God as judgmental has no effects at all.

CONCLUSION

Hell fire-and-brimstone sermons to the contrary, people respond far more strongly religiously to a carrot than to a stick. This has long been recognized by Christian missionaries: "For God so loved the world, that he gave his only begotten Son, that whosoever believeth in him should not perish, but have everlasting life. For God sent not his Son into the world to condemn the world; but that the whole world through him might be saved" (John 3:16-17 KJV).

Contributors: Christopher Bader and Paul Froese

EVIL

Did Sin Cause the Hurricane?

The existence of evil has always troubled theologians. How can God be omnipotent and loving and yet allow sin to exist and so often seem to triumph? Responses to this dilemma have long been the subject of theological and philosophical debate. The fourth-century British monk Pelagius argued that evil was a product of free will, which allowed the individual to knowingly engage in wicked deeds. His contemporary Augustine of Hippo contended that rather than electing to carry out evil, iniquity was inherent to human existence, an idea that came to be known as the doctrine of original sin.

Yet the uncomfortable implication that God is responsible for the existence of evil led some later thinkers to modify this characterization of evil. Writing in the nineteenth century, philosopher Arthur Schopenhauer maintained that people are themselves the creators of evil in the world, since morality and ethics do not exist outside the individual. More recently, American theologian Reinhold Niebuhr returned to the emphasis on original sin but modified the view that evil emanated in the individual, instead attributing the origin of evil to the nature of collective behavior.

Other attempts to reconcile the existence of evil with that of an omnipotent and benevolent God locate the source of evil in the existence of an antagonistic, malevolent spirit—Satan. In ancient Greco-Roman religions, the idea of a single personification of evil did not exist.[1] The concept of evil evolved in New Testament writings, which anthropomorphized Satan. According to biblical scholar Elaine Pagels, Satan became a device for Christians to demonize their enemies and more generally paint as evil those things which are in opposition to God. While this conclusion has its critics, it nevertheless resonates with the tendency to credit God when the outcome of a particular situation is approved of, and blame Satan when the outcome is disapproved.[2]

Such questions about the nature of evil extend beyond the ivory tower. In the formulation and maintenance of a moral framework, individuals must wrestle with the seemingly contradictory nature of the coexistence of evil and an omniscient and benevolent God. While questions about the nature of evil will persist unresolved in the academy, it is possible to better understand the role of specific perceptions of evil in the lives of everyday individuals. Further, as an important part of a larger worldview, such perceptions are likely to influence related moral and social attitudes.

PERCEPTIONS OF EVIL AND MORALITY

Perceptions of ultimate good and evil represent fundamental components in the foundation of a broader moral framework. An individual's understanding and conception of the nature of good and evil serve as core beliefs upon which specific moral attitudes are based and formulated. This perspective on the interconnectedness of beliefs with certain beliefs representing the core or foundation is best analogized to a web.[3] All able-minded humans are confronted with the outside world, both social and physical, which they must mentally process. As they operate within their environments they are confronted with a vast array of topics, options, and opportunities. Within this framework and day-to-day activity, people necessarily form beliefs on the vast array of information and experience presented to them. Some beliefs are held on the periphery of a person's web and will be easily discarded if necessary. Believing that the local pharmacy is open on Sunday is a loosely held belief— one that can be amended or confirmed with a phone call or car ride. Such peripheral beliefs have little impact on other beliefs. However, some attitudes occupy a position toward the center of the web, and consequently influence related beliefs that are built upon the core. These are beliefs about the very nature of the world in which people live. In this chapter, we seek to explore these inmost beliefs by investigating perceptions of evil.

A starting place for examining this topic is to assess where individuals attribute the source of evil: whether evil is caused by supernatural forces or humans, whether greed is the root of all evil, or whether all these sources are working in concert. Previous quantitative research has done little to address these questions. Research indicating that perceptions of ultimate good (such as images of God) are beliefs that deserve scholarly attention and influence a vast array of other moral and political attitudes is grow- ing rapidly. Perceptions of evil represent the flip side to percep- tions of ultimate good and are an important but overlooked aspect in our understanding of religious belief and its connection to other areas of social life. In an initial exploration of this topic, we exam- ine information on sociological patterns of belief in perceptions of evil. Similar to a person's image of God, we demonstrate that perceptions of evil hold significance beyond the religious sphere, bearing on both moral and political attitudes.

SOCIAL PATTERNS OF PERCEPTIONS OF EVIL

Previous research has provided limited information on perceptions of evil. The first wave of the Baylor Religion Survey (2005) tells us that roughly 58 percent of Americans absolutely believe in Satan while slightly fewer (48%) believe in demons. Further, women, African Americans, and those of lower income and education levels all report higher levels of belief in conceptions of supernatu- ral evil. However, measuring belief in the existence of supernatural evil does not directly provide information on whether respondents attribute evil in the world to these supernatural entities.

The Baylor Religion Survey 2007 includes a battery of questions addressing a respondent's perceptions of evil that probe this issue further. Respondents were instructed to indicate their level of agreement with specific statements about evil in the world. Four questions directly inquired about the nature of evil: "most evil in the world is caused by the devil," "most evil in the world is caused by mankind," and "human nature is basically evil."

TABLE 37
Sources of Evil

	Agree
Most evil in the world is caused by the devil.	43%
Most evil in the world is caused by mankind.	89%
Human nature is basically evil.	25%

Table 37 shows that belief in the existence of evil is widely held. Altogether, 94 percent of those who believe in evil locate its source in either the devil or mankind. Examined individually, roughly 43 percent of Americans agree or strongly agree that evil in the world is caused by the devil, indicating that many people attribute evil to supernatural forces. Belief in mankind as the source of evil is far less variable: 89 percent believe this to be true. These figures suggest that beliefs about the source of evil are not mutually exclusive views, as even those who attribute evil to the devil still believe mankind plays an active role in causing evil. Among those who believe that the devil is the source of most evil, 84 percent also attribute most evil to mankind. In short, *most* people believe that mankind is responsible for evil in the world. However, most people do not believe that human nature is basically evil.

TABLE 38
Sources of Evil and Denominations

	Devil causes evil	Mankind causes evil	Human nature causes evil
Conservative Protestants	73%	84%	39%
Liberal Protestants	34%	92%	17%
Roman Catholics	38%	90%	13%
Atheists	0%	88%	19%

When these perceptions are broken down according to religious tradition, greater variation in belief is evident. While the vast majority of conservative Protestants (73%) attribute evil to the devil, only about a third of liberal Protestants and Catholics do so. Not surprisingly, no atheists agree that Satan causes evil, and they overwhelmingly (88%) attribute evil to mankind. Although the great majority in each group believes that evil is caused by mankind, conservative Protestant respondents are a bit less likely to do so, suggesting that some of them do attribute evil solely to the supernatural. However, conservative Protestants (39%) are far more likely than the other religious groups to believe that human nature is basically evil, although only a minority of them do so.

• *Gender:* Women (47%) are more likely than men (39%) to attribute evil to the devil, while men (29%) exceed women (22%) in regarding human nature as basically evil. That women are more likely to attribute evil to supernatural forces is consistent with the fact that women tend to be more religious than men (see chapter 7). Meanwhile, men are more likely to have a pessimistic view of human nature.

• *Race:* African Americans (70%) are far more likely than whites (40%) to say that the devil causes evil, but there are no significant differences in views of human nature and evil.

- *Education:* People with only a high-school education or less (50%) are more apt to blame evil on the devil than are those who attended graduate school (26%).
- *Age:* Age has no effects.
- *Marital Status:* Married people (46%) are more likely to agree that the devil causes evil than are the divorced (35%), single (35%), and those living together (31%). Single people (38%) are the most likely to think human nature is evil, compared with 23 percent of married people and 12 percent of those living together.
- *Politics:* Conservatives (58%) are far more likely than liberals (21%) to blame the devil, and the same pattern holds (36% vs. 11%) on thinking human nature is basically evil. These figures reflect the well-known connection between religious and political conservatism.

PERCEPTIONS OF EVIL AND MORAL FRAMEWORKS

Basic conceptions of good and evil provide the base upon which more specific moral questions are understood. Further, how a person perceives good and evil provides an interpretive lens through which other questions of morality are viewed. As a glimpse of these possibilities, consider Table 39.

Both views of evil are related to being more punitive toward criminals. Those who blame evil on human nature and those who trace it to the devil are significantly less willing to abolish capital punishment and far more in favor of punishing criminals more harshly.

CONCLUSION

While debate about the theological and philosophical sources of evil will persist, the Baylor Religion Survey provides unique, national-level data on this previously understudied (from the perspective of social science) aspect of religious and moral perceptions. Analyses indicate that there are distinct social patterns regarding who is likely to hold certain perceptions of evil. Women are more likely to

TABLE 39
Human Nature Is Evil and Punishing Crime

"Human nature is basically evil."

	Agree	Disagree
The federal government should:		
"abolish the death penalty"	16%	26%
"punish criminals more harshly"	79%	67%

"Most evil in the world is caused by the devil."

	Agree	Disagree
The federal government should:		
"abolish the death penalty"	18%	30%
"punish criminals more harshly"	81%	59%

believe that the devil is the cause of evil, while men are more likely to believe that human nature is basically evil.

Here we have been content to show that there are interesting relationships between conceptions of the causes of evil and a variety of personal characteristics. But these data can surely offer an opportunity to explore far more fully whether (and how) beliefs about evil can serve as the foundation for one's broader moral framework, as is suggested by the strong connections to political identity and religious denomination. Our brief foray into the currently uncharted realm that is the sociological study of perceptions of evil suggests that these beliefs hold a key to understanding moral attitudes more generally.

Contributors: Joseph Baker and Ashley Palmer-Boyes

SPIRITUALITY
Religion and Spirituality Are Not Mutually Exclusive

"I have always been a spiritual person. I was once a very confused Catholic spiritual person, but I quickly discovered that my true spiritual happiness lies not in the organization and foundation of religion, but in the wide acceptance and tolerance afforded by the mixing of philosophies and beliefs." These words, expressed by a female in her twenties, present a fashionable but unfortunate contrast. Spirituality—expressed in personal, mystical, experiential terms—is pitted against religiousness, understood as institutionalized beliefs and practices including church membership, church attendance, and commitment to organizationally sanctioned doctrines.[1]

There seem to be many Americans who, like the young woman quoted above, have come to separate spirituality and religiousness, and by the 1990s this gave rise to the belief that spirituality is displacing religiosity. Consequently, scholars rushed to enumerate the growing proportions of spiritual Americans and to profile who they are. It soon was discovered that spirituality and religiousness are not separate constructs in the minds of many, perhaps most, Americans. They regard being spiritual as an integral part of being religious. Nevertheless, it was suggested that 18–20 percent of Americans did fit the description of spiritual, but not religious.[2] Most of these studies, however, employed non-probability samples, and some utilized forced choices that did not give respondents an option to choose both spiritual and religious to describe themselves. One of the few studies to make use of nationally representative survey data, drawing on the 1998 General Social Survey, discovered the estimate of spiritual-but not-religious people to be just 10 percent.[3]

Despite sampling limitations, a fair amount is now known about who these spiritual Americans are. In his book *Spiritual, but Not Religious*, Robert C. Fuller summarizes spiritual-but-not-religious people as "more likely than other Americans to have a college education, to belong to a white-collar profession, to be liberal in their political views, to have parents who attended church less frequently, and to be more independent in the sense of having weaker social relationships."[4] Other studies likewise find the spiritual-but-not-religious category to be related to age, ethnicity, region, marital status, education, income, service attendance, prayer, and parents' level of religious attendance when a respondent was a child.[5]

In all research, the quality of the data determines a lot about the quality of conclusions that emerge. Limited samples and surveys with limited religious content have hampered research on spirituality and religiousness. Our contribution is to use new national religion data to probe popular understandings of spirituality and religiousness. We offer a new look at the extent and implications of American spirituality.

The 2007 Baylor Religion Survey verifies that the terms "spiritual" and "religious" are both commonly used in the United States. Two-thirds of Americans (66%) say that the term "spiritual" describes them as very or somewhat well and three-fourths of Americans (74%) report that they are very or somewhat religious. When these self-assessed labels are combined, the results are these:

Spiritual, but not religious	10%
Spiritual and religious	57%

Religious, but not spiritual	17%
Neither	16%
	100%

These data show that, far from being mutually exclusive categories, spirituality and religiousness tend to largely overlap in the minds of Americans. In fact, more than half of American adults (57%) say they are both spiritual and religious. A much smaller minority, just 10 percent, are spiritual but not religious.

These two percentages match up closely with estimates from other nationally representative samples. Using the 1998 General Social Survey (GSS), Shahabi and a team of colleagues calculated the spiritual and religious group to be 52 percent and the spiritual-only group to be 10 percent.[6]

Who are the Americans who say they are spiritual, but not religious?

• *Gender*: Although women are more likely than men to be religious (see chapter 7) the genders are equally likely to claim to be spiritual, but not religious.

• *Race*: Whites and African Americans are equally likely to say they are spiritual, but not religious.

• *Age*: Age has a strong effect: 18 percent of Americans under thirty say they are spiritual, but not religious, compared with 16 percent of those 30–49, 6 percent of those 50–69, and 3 percent of those 70 and over.

• *Education*: Only 6 percent of those who did not attend college say they are spiritual, but not religious, compared with 12 percent of those who attended graduate school.

• *Marital Status*: Unwed people living together (26%) are most likely to say they are spiritual, but not religious, followed by the divorced (13%), single (12%), married (7%), and the widowed (6%).

• *Politics*: Republicans (5%) are less likely than Democrats (11%) to be spiritual, but not religious, while Independents (16%) top them both.

• *Region:* Western states (13%) are home to a larger percentage of people who say they are spiritual but not religious than other regions, the East (10%) is second, the Midwest (9%) is third, and the South (7%) is lowest.

• *Denomination:* Differences across the denominations are slight, which no doubt reflects the fact that most of these people have left organized religions.

TABLE 40

Conventional Religious Practices and Beliefs

	Spiritual only	Religious*
Church Attendance		
Weekly	14%	49%
Never	46%	9%
Prayer		
Daily	27%	62%
Seldom or never	45%	12%
Bible Reading		
Weekly or more often	13%	36%
Never	50%	14%
"The Bible is an ancient book of history and legends"	59%	11%
In your opinion, does each of the following exist (% absolutely)		
The devil/Satan	25%	67%
Heaven	33%	77%
Hell	23%	65%
Angels	69%	93%

* All who said they were religious persons

Consistent with the lack of denominational differences, most of the spiritual-only Americans have dropped out of conventional religion: few attend church, and prayer and Bible reading are not typical. Likewise, a substantial majority think the Bible is just a book and reject the existence of Satan, heaven, and hell. However, most of them do believe in angels. What else do the spiritual-only believe?

TABLE 41
Unconventional Beliefs and Identities

	Spiritual Only	Religious
Belief in God		
"I believe in a higher power or cosmic force."	44%	7%
Attributes of God (% absolutely or probably)		
Fatherly	50%	88%
A "He"	24%	55%
Angered by sin	31%	65%
In your opinion, does each of the following exist (% absolutely or probably)		
Ghosts	59%	50%
Extraterrestrials	63%	44%
Psychic phenomena such as ESP	77%	63%
Describe themselves as a (% very much or somewhat)		
Mystic	21%	9%
Contemplative	52%	37%
Theological liberal	35%	18%
"I have felt one with the universe."	42%	22%

A near majority of the spiritual-only respondents think of God as an impersonal higher power or cosmic force, and they are reluctant to consider God as a father or a "he." The overwhelming majority also deny that God (whatever they mean by the term) is angered by sin. On the other hand, it would be quite incorrect to assume they reject nonempirical beings and phenomena. Just as most of them believe in angels, so do they believe in ghosts, in extraterrestrials, and such things as ESP. They are far more likely than religious Americans to identify themselves as "mystics," as "contemplative" and as "theological liberals." They also are more apt to have felt themselves as being one with the universe.

The pattern that emerges from the data is of a spirituality that is privatized in the sense of not being anchored in formal organizations and nontraditional in terms of beliefs.[7] Those who consider themselves as "spiritua,l but not religious" reject two main orthodoxies. One is a materialistic worldview that denies supernatural reality, and the other is traditional religion, which has failed to provide them a sastifying spiritual experience. Thus, instead of relying on the routines of traditional religious practices and rituals, they take the approach of "spiritual eclecticism," being open to various nontraditional beliefs, such as parapsychology, New Age spirituality, and Eastern mystical philosophies.[8] Obviously, most of these spiritual-only Americans are involved in the New Age (see chapter 15), but since the New Age items were asked only in 2005 and the "spiritual" item only in 2007, we cannot demonstrate the connection.

What we can show, however, is that the spiritual-only respondents also are distinctive in terms of their opinions on some issues that are the focus of the so-called culture wars.

From Table 42 we can quite clearly see that spiritual-only Americans tend overwhelmingly to take the liberal side in the culture wars.

TABLE 42
Culture-War Issues

	Spiritual only	Religious
Approve of		
The use of marijuana	72%	35%
Homosexual marriage	68%	22%
Physician-assisted suicide	74%	34%
Women only:		
"I consider myself a feminist."	56%	26%

Finally, many observers have claimed that the existence of spiritual-only Americans represents an exodus from the conventional churches and, as such, may be a symptom of an impending decline of organized faiths.[9] This seems less likely when their religious origins are examined. Nearly half are the product of a mixed-religion marriage, and the great majority say they were not very religious at age 12—only 10 percent report having been "very religious." Hence, persons with devout religious backgrounds are not jettisoning religion for spirituality.

CONCLUSION

Several conclusions can be drawn from this overview of spirituality and religiousness in contemporary America. First, religion and spirituality are not mutually exclusive categories. Over half of present U.S. adults consider themselves to be both spiritual and religious. Second, what those who say they are spiritual, but not religious actually mean is that they reject the churches and the major religious traditions but cling to supernaturalism. Since their beliefs are not rooted in organized traditions, they tend to embrace all manner of unusual and paranormal claims. However, identifying themselves as spiritual allows these people to distance themselves from aspects of organized religion that they find displeasing without inheriting the stigmatized status of unbelief.[10] Put another way, while discarding what they reject in religion, they continue to be, in essence, "religious." As was recently pointed out, "spirituality" is a form of "unchurched religion."[11] So, except in a linguistic sense, it turns out that spirituality and religiousness are not so easily separated.

Contributors: Kevin Dougherty and Sung Joon Jang

GIVING

The Rich, the Poor, and the Widow's Mite

Tithing (from the Old English word for a tenth) has always aroused controversy among Christians. The Old Testament (Mal 3:8-12) sets an obligation on all Jews to contribute a tenth of their incomes to the temple, more often in kind than in cash. Eventually, tithing took the form of a mandatory religious tax imposed by the rulers of Israel. However, the New Testament is somewhat ambiguous as to tithing, and most Protestants have interpreted verses such as Matthew 23:23 and Luke 11:42 in opposition to a requirement to tithe and have, instead, emphasized free-will offerings. The Protestant view is consistent with the practice followed by the early church, which sustained no doctrine of tithing. Rather, Paul stressed cheerful giving (2 Cor 9:7) and giving what one can afford (2 Cor 8:3). Tithing as a required Christian church tax was initiated under Pope Adrian I in 787.

Mandatory church taxes are still collected in many European nations, including Austria, Denmark, Finland, Germany, Italy, and Sweden, but nowhere does tithing remain the standard—1 percent is now the typical church tax rate. Few seem aware of it, but there were mandatory church taxes in most of the American colonies. Following the Revolution, most states abolished church taxes, but it was not until 1833 that Massachusetts finally ceased collecting church taxes on behalf of the Congregationalists. Meanwhile, as mandatory church contributions have been fading away, some denominations have stressed the tithe as the standard for voluntary giving. How successful are they? Indeed:

Who gives money to the church?

How much do they give?

Who tithes?

Answers to these questions can be discovered by examination of the combined responses to two waves of the Baylor Survey taken in the winter of 2005 and the fall of 2007. Since it would be silly to explore the religious contributions of the unchurched, those who never attend church or who attend church less than once a year were excluded from the analysis. Among people who attend church at least once a year or more (which is 71.6 percent of the population), the average portion of income given to the church is 3.9 percent. As shown in Table 43, that average varies by household-income level.

TABLE 43
Religious Contributions by Income Level

Household income	Average dollar amount	Percent of income
[Annual contributions to place of worship]		
$10,000 or less	$572	11.4%
$10,001–$20,000	$927	6.2%
$20,001–$35,000	$1,269	4.6%
$35,001–$50,000	$1,410	3.3%
$50,001–$100,000	$2,010	2.7%
$100,001–$150,000	$2,767	2.2%
$150,001 or more	$4,083	2.7%

Not surprisingly, as income goes up, the average dollar amount donated also goes up. But the richer people are not the ones who give the highest percentage of income to their places of worship. Instead, lower-income people give a higher percentage of their income to the church. There is a slight upturn at the very highest level of income, suggesting that the relationship between contribution percentage and income may have a slight U-shape to it. Clearly, though, it is the "poor" who give the largest percentage of their incomes to the church.

As noted, different denominations place differing emphases on the importance of tithing, with more conservative churches stressing more heavily the duty to give a full 10 percent of income. For example, most churches in conservative and black Protestant denominations teach the importance of tithing to the church. Mormons require members to tithe but allow members to define how the tithe is calculated (whether of gross or net income, for example) and take an individual's word as to whether or not tithing was fulfilled. Table 44 shows the differences in contributions across religious traditions. Consistent with the greater emphasis on tithing, Mormons, black Protestants, and conservative Protestants give a higher percentage of their incomes to their churches compared to the other groups.

TABLE 44
Religious Contributions by Religious Tradition

	Average contribution	Percent per year of income	Percent donating 10% or more
Catholic	$1,064	2.2%	2.5%
Liberal Protestant	$1,598	3.0%	5.9%
Conservative Prot.	$2,396	5.5%	14.4%
Black Protestant	$1,978	5.7%	13.5%
Latter-day Saint (Mormon)	$4,159	7.1%	34.0%

Obviously, in no group are all, or even most, members giving a tenth of their incomes, including those groups that most emphasize tithing. But as Table 45 shows, the most active church-goers are also the highest percentage givers. Those who attend church several times a week come very close to contributing an average of 10 percent, and almost a third of the most active church-goers are donating at least 10 percent.

TABLE 45
Religious Contributions by Church-Attendance Level

Frequency of church attendance	Average contribution per year	Percent of income	Percent donating 10% or more
Several times a week	$3,481	9.5%	29.9%
Weekly	$2,666	5.1%	13.2%
About weekly	$1,879	3.5%	7.5%
2–3 times a month	$1,230	2.6%	3.7%
Once a month	$891	1.8%	1.2%
Several times a year	$708	1.8%	1.6%
Once or twice a year	$496	1.3%	0.7%

The final question we explore is whether there is a "widow's mite" effect. In the Gospel of Luke (21:2), Jesus praised a poor widow for giving her only two remaining copper coins ("mites" in the King James Version) to the temple treasury, while challenging a rich young man to give away all his possessions. We have seen above that in modern America, the richer church-goers do not give as much in percentage terms as those with lower incomes. But what about the widows? Do they still give their mites? The data show that they do.

Compared to the rest of the population, widows and widowers are much more likely to tithe. Overall, 17.6 percent of widowed people tithe, while only 8.6 percent of the nonwidowed population tithes. Among the widowed, the likelihood of tithing varies by gender, with 20.1 percent of the widows tithing, compared to 16.9 percent of the widowers. And as can be seen in Table 46, widows and widowers give less in dollar amount but more as a percentage of their (lower) incomes. The widow's mite lives on today.

TABLE 46
Religious Contributions by Widowed Status

Marital status	Average contribution per year	Percent of income
Widowed	$1,415	7.8%
Other	$1,978	4.7%

Sample is limited to people age 60 and over.

TABLE 47
Age and Income of Tithers

	Average household income		Average age of respondent	
	percentage donated		percentage donated	
	10% or more	Less than 10%	10% or more	Less than 10%
Catholic	$19,854	$69,943	61.8	50.8
Liberal Protestant	$35,797	$67,275	58.6	50.5
Conservative Prot.	$32,703	$61,198	54.0	46.1
Black Protestant	$32,437	$49,008	55.6	51.6
Latter-day Saints	$45,999	$68,116	43.6	41.2

Table 47 completes the picture of who tithes and who doesn't. The pattern we saw in Table 43 appears in each religious tradition: tithers have much lower household incomes than nontithers. We also see that tithers are older: across all denominations, the average age of all tithers is 54.1 years, compared to 48.8 for nontithers. Within particular religious traditions, the tithers are older on average than the nontithers—the smallest age gaps are among black Protestants and Mormons, both of which typically place a strong emphasis on tithing.

In all, not very many regular church-goers actually give a tithe to their churches—which is not news to most pastors and church business administrators. Those who do tithe are typically lower-income and older. And the example of the widow's mite continues to resonate: widows and (to a lesser extent) widowers give the highest percentage of their incomes to the church, and they are the members most likely to tithe.

Contributors: Charles M. North, Wafa Hakim Orman,
and Carl R. Gwin

PERSONALITY
Are We Hardwired for God?

Social scientists have often speculated that there might be something innate about individual religiousness. Obviously, the details of religious culture are transmitted socially, but are they rooted in an underlying biological component of the human makeup, independent of culture and society? That certainly would account for the fact that no irreligious society has ever been discovered and that even immense efforts by tyrannical states to create such a society have been such utter failures (see chapter 14).

As with many genetic traits such as height and hand-eye coordination, a biological predisposition for religion could vary considerably across individuals, consistent with the observed variations in individual religiousness. That may have been what Max Weber had in mind when he noted that some individuals are simply more religiously "musical" than others and identified "religious virtuosi" in a variety of different religious traditions.[1] More recently, Brian D'Onofrio and his colleagues provide very suggestive evidence that "religious attitudes and practices are moderately influenced by genetic factors."[2]

While the ultimate tests of such claims must be physiological, it is possible to contribute to the discussion by examining personality characteristics to see if a plausible case can be made for religion as a basic component of personality. In pursuit of significant evidence, the 2007 Baylor Religion Survey included an appropriate set of questions. As will be seen in this very preliminary report, our findings strongly suggest that religiousness is a unique and important component of human personality and therefore merits closer study by psychologists as well as other scientists.

Words as a Window into Personality

What adjectives would you use to describe yourself, a romantic partner, or co-worker (i.e., quiet, pious, loud, obnoxious, religious, spiritual)? Would others use those same words to describe you? According to the lexical hypothesis, the most important facets of personality are encoded as trait terms in most of the world's languages.[3] That is, the words we use to describe people provide a window into human personality. By scientifically studying the words people use to describe the self and others, we can better understand personality trait structure.

Gordon Allport—a Harvard psychologist who conducted early scientific studies on personality and character traits—was one of the first to simply count the many words in an unabridged English dictionary that could be used to distinguish one person from another.[4] The list of "personality" words reached almost eighteen thousand.[5] Could there possibly be over ten thousand personality traits? If not, how many personality traits are there? And finally, is religiousness-spirituality a basic personality trait?

The recent consensus among personality psychologists is that there are five basic dimensions of personality called the Big Five, and religiousness is not one of them.[6] The thousands of words people use across cultures to describe the self and others frequently fit on one of these dimensions: Openness to Experience, Conscientiousness, Extroversion, Agreeableness, and Neuroticism. The mnemonic OCEAN may help you remember the Big Five personality traits. These five personality dimensions can be explained as follows: *Openness* (artistic and deep versus uncreative and shallow); *Conscientiousness* (efficient and organized versus undependable and sloppy); *Extroversion* (talkative and active versus quiet and reserved); *Agreeableness* (kind and sympathetic versus critical and selfish), and *Neuroticism/Emotional Stability* (anxious and moody versus relaxed and calm).

HOW ABOUT RELIGIOUSNESS?

Beyond the Big Five personality components, researchers ponder other aspects of personality relevant to more specific aspects of our lives. For instance, people use a variety of words to describe the self and others, including words such as sexy or unattractive, feminine or masculine, perverted or chaste, religious, spiritual, pious, and so forth, yet these facets of personality are not represented on the Big Five. Due to the importance and salience of our sexual lives and identities, researchers developed a new taxonomy for sexuality description.[7] We propose that religious life requires similar attention.

While religious-spiritual terms often group together with words like trusting, cooperative, and sympathetic on the Agree-ableness dimension of the five-factor model, some personality theorists contend that religious-spiritual may be a sixth or seventh dimension of personality.[8] In response, we examined the associations between religiousness, the Big Five, and some personal beliefs and attitudes in order to better understand the importance of religiousness in the prediction of personal beliefs, attitudes, and ideology.

Consistent with the lexical hypothesis, 2007 Baylor Survey respondents rated the extent to which the term "religious" described them. This unique measure of religiosity is based purely on self-identification with the personal perception of religiousness and is conceptually distinct from religious behaviors such as church attendance and religious beliefs such as whether one interprets the Bible literally. Consequently, it taps an underlying dimension of religious self perception. In tandem with this measure of religious personality, we assessed the Big Five components of personality; respondents were asked to rate ten items listed separately (i.e., extroverted, quiet, critical, sympathetic, dependable, disorganized, anxious, calm, open to new experiences, and uncreative) using the sentence stem, "I see myself as _____ (strongly disagree, disagree, undecided, agree, strongly agree)." This 2007 Baylor Survey ten-item personality measure was patterned after a very brief scale developed by Gosling, Rentfrow, and Swann.[9]

The analysis of these data requires the use of a very simple statistical technique called correlation. It is used to determine the strength of the connection between any two measures, for example, between church attendance and belief in flying saucers. If for every change of value in one measure there is an equivalent change in the other, then the correlation between the two is perfect. For example, if every variation in church attendance is matched with a similar change in the belief in flying saucers, that would be a perfect correlation and would be expressed numerically by a correlation coefficient taking the value 1.0. If changes in the value of one measure produce no coherent pattern of change in the other measure, then they are said to be uncorrelated and in that instance the correlation coefficient would take the value 0.0.

Correlation coefficients can be either positive or negative. If an *increase* in church attendance is matched by a *decrease* in belief in flying saucers, that is a *negative* correlation. If the more church attendance, the more belief in flying saucers, or if the less of one, the less of the other, that is a *positive* correlation. In the real world there are many things that are uncorrelated, but perfect correlations (1.0) are extremely rare. Hence, correlation coefficients usually fall somewhere between 0.0 and 1.0. That raises questions about how high a value should be before it is regarded as real, as opposed to simply reflecting chance—random variations resulting from "luck" and unlikely to happen again. Tests of statistical significance are calculations of the odds that an observed correlation was not produced by change but reflects a real connection between two measures. All of this can be observed in Table 48.

TABLE 48

Correlations between Personality Measures and Religious Practices

	Self-reported religiosity	Extroversion	Agreeableness	Conscientious	Emotional stability	Openness to new experiences
Church attendance	.492**	.019	.133**	.020	.063*	-.028
Read Bible, Koran, or Torah outside religious services	.533**	-.018	.154**	-.007	.121**	.004
Pray outside religious services	.458**	.001	.198**	.010	.051*	.029
Religious experiences	.371**	.055**	.146**	-.019	.030	.111**

* 20 to 1 odds against correlation being the result of random chance.
** Odds are greater than 1,000 to 1 that correlation is not the result of random chance.

Here we can see by reading down the first column that the measure of self-reported religiosity is positively associated with four religious practices—church attendance, reading of sacred texts outside of religious services, praying outside of religious services, and religious experiences. The highest correlation coefficient is .533 and the lowest is .371 (when there is no negative sign the correlation is positive). Notice the two asterisks beside each correlation coefficient in this column. That indicates the level of statistical significance. Two asterisks mean that the odds are greater than 1,000 to 1 that this correlation was not the result of random chance. When there is only one asterisk, that means the odds against random chance are greater than 20 to 1. The calculation of significance is based not only on the value of the correlation coefficient but also on the number of "observations" on which it is based, in this instance on the more than 1,400 people in the survey. Notice, however, that even though these results are highly significant, the correlations are far from perfect. Clearly, then, there is more to one's self-perceived religiosity than simply faithfully observing the norms of one's religious community.

Notice, too, that except for the much lower, but still significant, correlations with the agreeableness dimension, the other measures of the Big Five are pretty much uncorrelated with the four religious behaviors. As for agreeableness, past research concerning the relationship between personality and religious commitment suggests a connection between religious practice and understanding oneself as a kind and sympathetic person.[10] Of course, it remains unclear whether participation in religion leads one to possess character qualities such as kindness and sympathy or if people who are kind and sympathetic by nature are more likely to enjoy religious activities. Perhaps both.

Table 49 reports correlations between personality dimensions and religious beliefs. Biblical literalism, certainty of God, and certainty of heaven reflect traditional beliefs, whereas certainty of ghosts, certainty of extraterrestrials, and certainty of psychic phenomenon reflect paranormal beliefs (see chapter 15). Self-defined

TABLE 49

Correlations between Personality Measures and Personal Beliefs

	Self-reported religiosity	Extraversion	Agreeableness	Conscientious	Emotional stability	Openness to new experiences
Biblical literalism	.314**	-.014	.085**	.010	.088**	-.075**
Certainty of God	.281**	.029	.129**	.021	.020	-.092**
Certainty of heaven	.306**	.020	.109**	-.017	.030	-.095**
Certainty of ghosts	-.198**	.039	.000	-.025	-.096**	.044
Certainty of extraterrestrials	-.200**	.044	-.018	-.053*	-.064*	.070**
Certainty of psychic phenomenon	-.227**	.066**	.002	-.060*	-.070**	.057*

* 20 to 1 odds against correlation being the result of random chance.

** Odds are greater than 1,000 to 1 that correlation is not the result of random chance.

religiosity is the only personality trait to be correlated significantly with all six beliefs. Those who are more religious are more likely to report biblical literalism, certainty of God, and certainty of heaven. However, the other three correlations are negative. The more religious persons reported being, the less likely they were to be certain of ghosts, extraterrestrials, and psychic phenomenon. These findings demonstrate what we will see in chapter 15, that religious people are less likely to accept paranormal beliefs and that those who accept such beliefs tend not to view themselves as "religious." Again, agreeableness correlates significantly (but weakly) with the traditional religious beliefs but is unrelated to paranormal beliefs.

Table 50 displays the correlations between personality measures and various moral attitudes. These moral-attitude items are much broader in scope than the personal-belief items. Participants were asked to what degree they believe the following are wrong: abortion (if the family cannot afford the child), divorce (if children are present), marijuana use, physician-assisted suicide, embryonic-stem-cell research, and war. Responses were given on a four-point scale (always wrong, almost always wrong, only wrong sometimes, or not wrong at all); lower scores indicate that people oppose the behavior more strongly. With the exception of war, self-reported religiosity is positively related to viewing each of these issues as immoral.

Similarly, agreeableness is positively correlated with all of these items, although the relationships are weaker than those of self-reported religiosity. In other words, individuals who see themselves as kind and sympathetic are more likely to view all of these behaviors as immoral, including war.

Interesting to note is that extroversion and openness to new experiences work in opposition to religiosity and agreeableness. Individuals possessing these personality traits are less likely to view the list of issues as immoral. Perhaps this also reflects the willingness of individuals to engage in these activities, as prior research has shown that those who are more open to new experiences are

TABLE 50

Correlations between Personality Measures and Moral Attitudes

Immorality of:	Self-reported religiosity	Extroversion	Agreeableness	Conscientious	Emotional stability	Openness to new experiences
Abortion, if the family cannot afford the child	.304**	-.062*	.094**	-.003	.056*	-.082**
Divorce, if children are present	.275**	-.082**	.053*	-.026	.054*	-.063*
Use of marijuana	.271**	-.076**	.096**	.060*	.084**	-.122**
Physician-assisted suicide	.349**	-.070**	.079**	.027	.074	-.056*
Embryonic-stem-cell research	.349**	-.067**	.059*	.015	.055*	-.039
War	-.073*	-.063*	.088**	-.040	-.060*	.028

* 20 to 1 odds against correlation being the result of random chance.

** Odds are greater than 1,000 to 1 that correlation is not the result of random chance.

TABLE 51
Correlations between Personality Measures and Political Identity

	Self-reported religiosity	Extroversion	Agreeableness	Conscientious	Emotional stability	Openness to new experiences
Liberal	-.276**	.039	.008	-.066**	-.079**	.102**
Democrat	-.157**	-.018	.062*	-.035	-.023	.056*

* 20 to 1 odds against correlation being the result of random chance.

** Odds are greater than 1,000 to 1 that correlation is not the result of random chance.

more likely to use marijuana.[11] Nevertheless, religiosity proves to be the strongest predictor of moral attitudes, stronger than any other personality trait.

Table 51 reports the correlations between the personality measures and political identity (a liberal-conservative scale and a Democrat-Republican scale). Of all the personality measures, religiosity shows the strongest correlation with these markers of political identity. Individuals who view themselves as religious are less likely to think of themselves as liberal and also less likely to be members of the Democratic Party. Openness to new experiences is the only other personality dimension that correlates strongly with both political identities. The more open a person is, the more likely he or she is to be liberal and a Democrat.

CONCLUSION

These data reveal that religiosity has a strong relationship with personal beliefs, moral attitudes, and political identity. Not only does religiosity correlate more strongly with these various beliefs, behaviors, and identities than any of these personality traits, but it also correlates consistently with all of them. Thus, religiosity seems to be as important, if not more so, as general personality traits in predicting these important aspects of social life.

One must note, however, that both moral attitudes and political identities carry with them issues that are religiously driven. In fact, religion's role in politics and political decisions is becoming increasingly more direct.[12] With an ongoing influence on politics and morality, religion strongly supports certain views on hotly debated topics such as embryonic-stem-cell research and abortion. Additionally, the Bible (as well as other sacred texts) speaks out directly on a variety of moral issues. Self-reported religiosity also appears related to traditional forms of religion but not paranormal beliefs. That is, individuals view themselves as personally religious to the extent that they practice conventional religious behaviors and hold mainstream religious beliefs.

In sum, evidence from the Baylor Religion Survey supports the conclusion that religiosity is a uniquely important dimension of personality. Although these data may not tell us whether religiosity is a sixth or seventh dimension of personality, they do suggest that religiosity provides unique explanatory power when included with measures of general personality. As such, religiosity should be taken into consideration when examining individual differences in personal beliefs and moral attitudes. More importantly, the idea that religiousness reflects a unique personality, emotional, or relational factor is a serious possibility that has not received appropriate scientific attention. If that were to turn out to be true, it would help explain why religion is so universal.

Contributors: Megan Johnson, Jordan LaBouff,
Paul Froese, and Wade Rowatt

Part III

ATHEISM AND IRRELIGION

ATHEISM
The Godless Revolution That Never Happened

For several centuries, Western intellectuals have been predicting the death of religion. Writing in about 1710, the English freethinker Thomas Woolston (1670–1731) expressed his confidence that religion would be gone by 1900. Voltaire (1694–1778) thought Woolston was being far too pessimistic and suggested that the end of religion would come within the, then, next fifty years.[1]

The failure of these early prophesies had no deterrent effects. Thus, the distinguished Max Müller (1823–1900) complained in his Hibbert Lectures of 1878: "Every day, every week, every month, every quarter, the most widely read journals seem just now to vie with each other in telling us that the time for religion is past, that faith is a hallucination or an infantile disease, that the gods have at last been found out and exploded."[2]

By the 1960s this perspective dominated the social sciences. Thus, according to the very distinguished anthropologist Anthony F. C. Wallace, in his very popular undergraduate textbook: "The evolutionary future of religion is extinction. Belief in supernatural beings and in supernatural forces that affect nature without obeying nature's laws will erode and become only an interesting memory . . . belief in supernatural powers is doomed to die out, all over the world, as a result of the increasing adequacy and diffusion of scientific knowledge . . . the process is inevitable."[3]

At about the same time, the well-known sociologist Peter Berger told *The New York Times* that by "the 21st century, religious believers are likely to be found only in small sects, huddled together to resist a worldwide secular culture . . . the predicament of the believer is increasingly like that of a Tibetan astrologer on a prolonged visit to an American university."[4] In light of the recent lionization of the Dalai Lama by the American media and his cordial welcome on many campuses, Berger's simile now admits to an ironic interpretation. And, in fact, in 1997 Berger gracefully took it all back, noting that, if anything, the world had gotten more religious during the interim.

Surprisingly, these predictions of the end of religion never attracted much attention outside of narrow academic circles, and most believers never knew they were supposed to be the last of the lot. But, in the past several years an explosion of popular books by angry and remarkably nasty atheists has hit the bestseller list:

The God Delusion by Richard Dawkins (2006)
Breaking the Spell by Daniel C. Dennett (2006)
God Is Not Great: How Religion Poisons Everything by Christopher Hitchens (2007).

As for nasty: Dawkins charged that teaching children about religion ought to be recognized as "child abuse" and outlawed. Dennett refers to atheists as "brights" in contrast with those dullards who still cling to faith. And all three authors propose that just about every brutal moment in history was caused by religion—remarkably they avoid acknowledging that the twentieth century was the bloodiest in history because of antireligious tyrants: Hitler, Stalin, and Mao.

Because these books sold well, it was widely assumed that they signaled a breakthrough for atheism—that large numbers of Americans were now ready to stand up and admit they didn't believe in God. That seemed to be confirmed by claims that the number of Americans who say they have no religious affiliation had climbed sharply in recent years[5] (the Baylor Surveys placed their number at 11 percent). But this "evidence" soon crumbled because those making this claim were so careless that they hadn't bothered to check on the actual religiousness of those who report having no religion. It turns out that the majority of them pray and the great majority are not atheists.[6] Apparently, what most people who say that they have no religion mean is not that they are irreligious, but that they have no church (see chapter 17).

So, what about atheists? Is their number growing? Table 52 shows that during the past sixty-three years, the percentage of atheists hasn't changed at all.

TABLE 52
Percent of Those Who Do Not Believe in God by Year

1944 (Gallup)	4%
1947 (Gallup)	6%
1964 (*American Piety*)	3%
1994 (GSS)	3%
2005 (Baylor Survey)	4%
2007 (Baylor Survey)	4%

One reason the percentage of atheists has not grown during the past sixty years is that irreligion is not effectively transmitted from parents to children. Studies show that the majority of children born into an irreligious home end up joining a religious group—most often a conservative denomination.[7]

Nor is it only in the United States that atheists are scarce and where their numbers are not growing. Despite the fact that Americans are far more religious than people in most other advanced industrial nations, atheism has failed to take hold in these other nations as well, as is shown in Table 53.

TABLE 53
Atheism around the World (World Values Surveys, 2001–2002)

	Percent "I am a convinced atheist."
Canada	4%
New Zealand	5%
Australia	5%
Western Europe	
Austria	2%
Ireland	2%
Italy	3%
Iceland	3%
Finland	3%
Portugal	3%
Switzerland	4%
Norway	4%
Greece	4%
Denmark	5%
Great Britain	5%
Netherlands	6%
Sweden	6%
Spain	6%
Germany	7%
Belgium	7%
France	14%
Former Soviet bloc	
Poland	1%
Romania	1%
Georgia	1%
Ukraine	3%
Latvia	3%
Russia	4%

Slovakia	4%
Hungary	5%
Albania	5%
Bulgaria	6%
Czech Republic	8%
Asia	
Taiwan	2%
India	4%
Japan	12%
China	14%*

* National Survey, 2007 by Horizon Research Consultancy Group, Ltd.

An immense amount has been written about irreligious and secularized Europeans. But atheists they are not. Even in France, famous for its anticlerical and antireligious politics, only 14 percent say they do not believe in God. As for "godless" Finland and Iceland, 3 percent say they are atheists, precisely the same as in "priest ridden" Italy.

China is the only nation with as many atheists as France—14 percent. Partly that reflects a long tradition of "Godless" folk magic. But it also reflects the brutal persecution of those suspected of being religious believers that was sustained by the Maoist regime and that continues today to some extent, as will be discussed later.

By far the most interesting data in this table are those for the former Soviet bloc. For more than seventy years atheists controlled the Soviet state and enforced an official policy of atheism. Beginning in the first year of school, and each year all the way through college, students in the Soviet Union were required to take a course in atheism. Following World War II, when the Soviets took control of the nations of Eastern Europe, a similar system of atheist education was imposed. Year after year, students were rehearsed in all the angry antireligious arguments to be found in recent tracts such as Richard Dawkins' *The God Delusion*.

And it wasn't merely education that atheism had going for it in the Soviet bloc. There was intense discrimination against religious people—if you wanted to have a good job, you professed atheism. If you were too intensely or too overtly religious, you might get sent to a hard-labor camp or even be killed. The result? In Russia itself the score is: God 96 percent, atheism 4 percent, precisely the same as in the United States. Nor did the atheism campaign do significantly better anywhere in the rest of the old Soviet bloc.

In his very recent book, *The Plot to Kill God: Findings from the Soviet Experiment in Secularization*,[8] Paul Froese demonstrates the utter ineptitude of the Soviet efforts to instill atheism. In part the educational program made no progress because it was staffed by, and the teaching materials were prepared by, people who knew next to nothing about religion. The assumption was that since religion is nonsense, there is nothing much one needs to know to refute it. Hence, what the atheism faculty regarded as unanswerable criticisms of faith were, in fact, quite elementary matters of theology and easily refuted by the average church-goer.

This same effort to instill atheism by force prevailed in China except that the target was primarily the gods of the folk religions and Taoism, since these were the dominant religions—the Communist Party having decided to pretend that Confucianism was a philosophy, not a religion, and therefore did not (usually) persecute its priests. Unlike the Soviets, however, the Chinese made less effort at education, relying more on angry propaganda and brutal persecution. But the results were much the same. A recent poll of China showed that atheists are hugely outnumbered by those who believe in God(s), and as repression has waned, there has emerged a tidal wave of conversions to Christianity.

The ineptitudes of Soviet (and Chinese) attacks on religion also dominate the current crop of books on atheism. To expect to learn anything about important theological problems from Richard Dawkins or Daniel Dennett is like expecting to learn about medieval history from someone who had only read *Robin Hood*. This criticism has been expressed by many reviewers, even by those who are themselves atheists. Thus, the biologist H. Allen Orr, writing in the *New York Review of Books*, noted that he had once called Richard Dawkins a "professional atheist," but "I'm forced after reading his book [*The God Delusion*], to conclude that he's actually more of an amateur."[9] And, writing in the *London Review of Books*, the Marxist literary scholar Terry Eagleton dismissed Dawkins' characterization of religious beliefs as such silliness that "not even the dim-witted clerics who knocked me about in grammar school thought like that."[10]

So why have books by angry atheists been selling well? For one thing, 4 percent of the population of 300 million Americans amounts to more than 12 million people—a lot of them potential book buyers. For another thing, this 4 percent is greatly over-represented in the media, especially among book reviewers, and so the books received maximum coverage. But perhaps most of all, as Michael Novak suggested in a very perceptive article, both the authors and their readers may be animated, not by confidence that their time has come, but by despair. As Novak put it, "there is an odd defensiveness about all these books—as though they were a sign not of victory but of desperation."[11]

Novak's perceptions are confirmed by a very recent study based on interviews with people prominent in atheist organizations. Many expressed sentiments consistent with the idea that it is frustration for the lack of growth that has produced these angry outbursts—that American atheists have come to feel like embattled members of a very unfashionable, unpopular religious sect.[12] Fully in keeping with this conclusion, as shown in chapter 20, compared with other people, atheists are not comfortable talking about religion with their neighbors or co-workers. In fact, they tend to be uncomfortable talking about religion even with their friends and their families. And more than half agree that "My religious views are often ridiculed by the media."

That raises the question: Who are the atheists? Turning to the Baylor Surveys:

• *Education*: Atheists are better educated than other Americans, 28 percent of them having a graduate degree, compared with 16 percent of nonatheists, and nearly all of the atheists have attended college. But even among the graduate educated, atheists are a tiny minority of only 8 percent.

• *Income*: Atheists are a bit more likely to be in the upper-income brackets, but a bit less than would be expected on the basis of their educational advantages.

• *Gender*: Atheists are overwhelmingly male—73 percent. Seven percent of males are atheists, compared with 2 percent of females.

• *Race*: In the 2005 Baylor sample, of 133 African Americans there was not a single atheist.

• *Age*: There are no statistically significant differences in age between atheists and believers, which is consistent with there being no increases over time.

• *Family background*: There is a highly significant effect as to when atheists became irreligious: fifty-three percent say they were not religious at age twelve and only 8 percent reported that they had been very religious at age twelve. This is consistent with the fact that 31 percent of atheists had parents who also were irreligious. In addition, atheists are quite disproportionately from Jewish homes: 11 percent of those with Jewish parents say they are atheists, compared with 3 percent from Protestant and Catholic homes. But, of course, given the greater proportion of Protestants in the population, most atheists come from Protestant backgrounds.

• *Marital Status*: There are no significant differences between atheists and believers in terms of their marital status.

• *Politics*: Atheists are overwhelmingly on the political left. Nine percent identify themselves as Republicans, 46 percent as Democrats, 29 percent as Independents, and 16 percent with a third party, most of them being Libertarians.

To sum up: the average American atheist is a white, male, liberal ex-Protestant of any age, who has attended college.

CONCLUSION

During the early and middle decades of the twentieth century, the future seemed to belong to atheism. In the Soviet bloc and in China the school systems systematically taught that the discovery of historical materialism had revealed that God is an illusion or a hoax. Even many American textbooks claimed that atheism was the enlightened wave of the future. Moreover, in Communist nations, atheistic education was combined with repression of churches and believers—sometimes extremely brutal, as when the Red Army nailed Russian priests to their church doors and left them to freeze to death. Nearly three thousand priests were shot in 1918 alone.[13] Even so, the Godless Age never dawned.

15

CREDULITY
Who Believes in Bigfoot?

Twenty-eight years ago, two sociologists[1] provoked consternation among the readers of a humanist-sponsored magazine by reporting that in their large sample of college students those who said they were irreligious were the ones by far the most likely to embrace a series of occult and paranormal beliefs, while students who said they had been "born again" and that their religious beliefs were "very important" to them were by far those least likely to accept these beliefs.

Although the sociologists refrained from quoting the famous quip that when people stop believing in God they are ready to believe in anything, scores of readers of the *Skeptical Inquirer* wrote angry letters to the editors and directly to the authors to assert that such a finding could not possibly be true. But it was. For example, the irreligious were almost three times as likely as were the most religious students to place "great value" in "Tarot reading, séances, and psychic healing," Or, two-thirds of the irreligious agreed that "UFOs are probably real spaceships from other worlds," compared with only 40 percent of the most religious students. So, the essay concluded, "Those who hope that a decline in traditional religion would inaugurate a new Age of Reason ought to think again."

Opponents of these results made much of the fact that the data were based on 1,439 undergraduates at the University of Washington and therefore that the results probably (or most certainly) were peculiar to that institution or area. Moreover, many critics noted that, given a student sample, it was impossible to examine correlations between education and paranormal beliefs, and surely these would show "enlightened" effects. Subsequently, several studies have explored educational effects but with very mixed results—education was negatively correlated with some paranormal beliefs and positively related to others.[2] The same studies also had mixed results as to the link between conventional religiousness and belief in the paranormal. But all of these studies were either based on samples as odd as those used in the original study or were deficient in other ways. What has been needed is proper analysis of a good data set, using well-designed questions and scales.

Consequently, the Baylor Survey of 2005 included the following set of statements:

Dreams sometimes foretell the future or reveal hidden truths.

Agree	53%
Undecided	17%
Disagree	30%

Ancient advanced civilizations, such as Atlantis, once existed.

Agree	43%
Undecided	30%
Disagree	27%

Places can be haunted.

Agree	37%
Undecided	16%
Disagree	47%

It is possible to influence the physical world through the mind alone.

Agree	29%
Undecided	22%
Disagree	49%

Some UFOs are probably spaceships from other worlds.

Agree	24%
Undecided	27%
Disagree	49%

It is possible to communicate with the dead.

Agree	18%
Undecided	19%
Disagree	63%

Creatures such as Bigfoot and the Loch Ness Monster will one day be discovered by science.

Agree	17%
Undecided	27%
Disagree	56%

Astrology impacts one's life and personality.

Agree	14%
Undecided	15%
Disagree	71%

Astrologers, palm readers, tarot-card readers, fortune-tellers, and psychics can foresee the future.

Agree	12%
Undecided	15%
Disagree	73%

(The responses have been collapsed from the five categories offered to the respondents: Strongly agree, Agree, Disagree, Strongly disagree, and Undecided).

There is substantial belief in all nine of these items. Only a minority of Americans disagree with the first five items, a bare majority reject Bigfoot and the Loch Ness Monster, with the astrology items enlisting the least support. The items were summed to create an Index of Occult and Paranormal Belief. For purposes of this chapter, the Index was separated into quartiles—that is, cutting points were selected that put about 25 percent of the respondents in each of these categories: Low, Medium, Medium High, and High.

Many factors influence belief in the occult and paranormal.

• *Gender:* Women are substantially more likely than men to believe in the paranormal and occult: 20 percent of men scored high compared with 35 percent of women.

• *Race:* African Americans (41% high) are more likely than whites (26%) to believe.

• *Age:* Those under thirty are most likely to score high (40%), and those over sixty are least likely (17%), but there is no variation among the other age groups.

• *Marital Status:* Married people are least apt to score high (22%), compared with 40 percent of the never married and 49 percent who are living with someone.

• *Region:* The regional effect is barely significant: the East is highest (34%) and the South is lowest (24%).

• *Politics:* Party politics matters a lot. Only 16 percent of "strong" Republicans scored high compared with 40 percent of strong Democrats. Nineteen percent of Bush voters scored high compared with 34 percent of Kerry voters and 53 percent of those who favored Ralph Nader in the 2004 presidential elections.

• *Education:* Amazingly, the effect of education is barely significant: 28 percent of those with high school or less scoring high compared with 23 percent of those with post-graduate degrees.

Now let us turn to religion.

• *Church attendance* has a powerful, negative effect on belief in the occult and paranormal: 31 percent who never attend church scored high; only 8 percent who go more than once a week scored high.

• *Denomination* also matters: 31 percent of all liberal Protestants scored high, including 48 percent of Unitarians, 41 percent of Episcopalians, and 36 percent of those belonging to the United Church of Christ. In contrast, 18 percent of all Conservative Protestants scored high, including 14 percent of members of the Assemblies of God and 17 percent of Baptists. Catholics (32%) resemble liberal Protestants and Mormons (15%) resemble conservative Protestants.

• *Those who frequently witness* to or share their faith with strangers are far less apt to score high (9%) than are those who never do so (30%).

Still, it remains widely believed, especially among the media and social scientists, that religious people are especially credulous, especially those who identify themselves as Evangelicals, born again, Bible believers, fundamentalists, and the like. Let's see about that.

Respondents were offered a whole set of terms to describe their religious identity, including those just mentioned. Table 54 shows the results.

TABLE 54
Religious Self-Identity and Belief in the Occult and Paranormal

	Percent high on the index	
Evangelical	14%	Not: 30%
Born again	18%	Not: 31%
Fundamentalist	17%	Not: 29%
Bible-believing	23%	Not: 32%
Theologically conservative	13%	Not: 31%
Theologically liberal	40%	Not: 26%

All these differences are highly statistically significant and show precisely what the student data showed many years ago.

Those who identify themselves with various forms of traditional Christianity are far less likely to believe in the occult and paranormal than are other Americans. For example, of those who regard themselves as Evangelicals, 14 percent scored high, compared with 30 percent of those who reject this label. Now look at the last entry in the table. Those who identify themselves theologically as liberals (40%) are far more likely than other Americans (26%) to believe in the occult and paranormal. It is not religion in general that suppresses such beliefs, but conservative religion.

This difference turns up in many other ways. For example:

• People who never visit a Christian bookstore are far more likely to score high (32%) than those who visit such a store monthly (3%).

• People who never visit a New Age or metaphysical bookstore are far less likely to score high (25%) than are those who visit often (72%).

• People who have read any book in the Left Behind series are much less apt to score high (17%) than those who have not read one (30%).

• People who have read *The Purpose-Driven Life* are less likely to score high (19%) than those who have not read it (30%).

• People who have read any book on dianetics are more likely to score high (38%) than those who have not read any such book (27%).

• People who have read *The Da Vinci Code* are a bit more likely to score high (31%) than those who have not read it (25%)—the difference is statistically significant.

CONCLUSION

The findings are clear and strong. Traditional Christian religion greatly decreases credulity, as measured by beliefs in the occult and paranormal. In contrast, education has hardly any effect.

Clearly, then, those who lump all sorts of religious and paranormal beliefs into one package labeled "superstitions" are as wrong as those who see no difference between Christian and New Age bookstores. Whatever one may wish to say about the nonempirical character of such beliefs, they are not all cut from the same cloth. Rather, it seems that the choice is either to believe in the Bible or in Bigfoot. Moreover, for those concerned about shielding young people from the prevalent occult and paranormal beliefs in our society, the more certain "solution" seems not to be to send them to college, but to a conservative Sunday school.

Contributors: Christopher Bader and Carson Mencken

New Age Adherents
Well-Educated, Formerly Irreligious Elites

For years, the sociology of religion was stuck with a fallacy about new religious movements—that they always arise from lower-class protest and discontent. This claim derived from Marx' dismissal of religion as the "opium of the people" by way of the American Protestant theologian-turned-sociologist H. Richard Niebuhr, who proposed a cyclical theory to account for the proliferation of American denominations. Echoing Marx, Niebuhr claimed that a new religious movement is always "the child of an outcast minority, taking its rise in the religious revolts of the poor."[1] However, if a religious movement grows and becomes successful, he argued, inevitably it is taken over by the more privileged classes and soon deserts the lower classes, no longer providing them with an "opiate." At that point the poor are driven to form a new religious movement which, if it succeeds, will in its turn be captured and transformed by the privileged. Thus, where freedom of religion exists, there will also exist an endless cycle of the formation and transformation of religious groups. This is sometimes identified as the sect-to-church cycle.

It turns out that this entire thesis is simply wrong. A few movements may have been founded by the poor and dispossessed (perhaps some in the rural American South), but all of the well-known examples were in fact founded by the privileged. For example, although Niebuhr gave extended attention to the Methodists as an example of a proletarian religious movement, John Wesley and his colleagues did not depart from the Church of England and found Methodism because they were lower-class dissidents who wanted a faith that would compensate them for their poverty. They were themselves young men of privilege who began to assert their preference for a higher-intensity faith while at Oxford. By the same token, the prophets of the Old Testament all belonged "to the landowning nobility."[2] So did the Essenes, and contrary to tradition, early Christianity was also an elite movement.[3] What seems to be the case is that *religious movements usually are formed by people of privilege, especially those who inherited their status, who find that power and privilege do not satisfy spiritual concerns.* Thus, for example, Buddha was a prince, and fifty-five of his first sixty converts were of the nobility as were 75 percent of the ascetic medieval Catholic saints.[4]

There is a second basis for the prominence of privileged people in founding and joining new religious movements: early adopters of new ideas (and technologies) always come overwhelmingly from the ranks of the privileged, those having more education and expansive social networks. This line of analysis has been successfully applied to several new religious movements.[5]

Historically speaking, the New Age movement represents a relatively recent set of ideas in the American religious marketplace. While some argue that its origins were in the nineteenth-century spiritualist movement, most students of American religion identify the New Age movement as having arisen during the 1960s and attribute its formation to wealthy socialites (such as Laurence Rockefeller), many of them participants in the Esalen Institute at Big Sur, California.[6] The primary aspects of the New Age movement are an emphasis on personal spirituality and mystical feelings, on seeking inspiration from Eastern religions, on alternative medicine such as acupuncture and herbalism, suspicion of science, and the rejection of formal (rational) theology as represented by Christianity and Judaism.

The New Age movement is still quite new, and it remains an unconventional belief system in the United States. Hence, it ought still to be dominated by privileged people who were adrift from the conventional faiths. Conversely, it ought not to appeal to people, privileged or not, who are committed to a conventional religious perspective. Indeed, being an active member of a congregation embeds individuals in a network of friends and family members who are apt to frown upon experimenting with new religious ideas. Whether they do depends upon the character of the religious group to which they belong. Some denominations place very little emphasis on doctrine and permit very great latitude in what members, including the clergy, may avow. It is not unusual for members and clergy of such denominations to be active participants in and consumers of New Age groups and ideas. Indeed, this seems to reflect their search for spirituality and a sense of the supernatural that is lacking in their "home" denominations. However, New Age participation is unlikely for active members of more traditional denominations, both Christian and Jewish. One is very unlikely to find Baptists or Orthodox Jews at New Age gatherings—such people do not go out seeking faith but are content that they have found it.

Unfortunately, all discussions of who participates or even dabbles in New Age are based on casual impressions, not on systematic evidence. Consequently, in preparing wave one of the 2005 Baylor Religion Survey, six questions were included to plumb involvement in New Age thinking:

How many times in the past year did you visit a New Age/metaphysical bookstore?

Once or more	10%
Never	90%

How many times in the past year did you purchase something from a New Age/metaphysical bookstore?

Once or more	7%
Never	93%

Have you ever read a book, consulted a Web site or researched the New Age movement in general?

Yes	12%
No	88%

Have you ever read a book, consulted a Web site or researched specific techniques for spiritual development, such as yoga?

Yes	25%
No	75%

As an adult, have you ever used acupuncture or other forms of non-traditional medicine?

Yes	28%
No	72%

Have you ever read a book, consulted a Web site or researched alternative medicine?

Yes	50%
No	50%

Half of Americans have checked out alternative medicine, but only a quarter (28%) have used acupuncture or another form of nontraditional medicine. About the same number have read about yoga or some other spiritual technique. As for specific references to New Age thinking, only 12 percent have checked out the New Age movement in general. Ten percent have visited a New Age bookstore during the past year, and 7 percent have made a purchase in a New Age bookstore during the past year.

These six items are quite intercorrelated, so it is legitimate to combine them into a New Age Index, scored from 0 (no to all six items) to 6 (yes to all six items). Only 3 percent of Americans scored 6, so the index was collapsed as follows:

Zero	38%
Low (1)	27%
Medium (2)	18%
High (3–6)	17%
	100%

Table 55 demonstrates the validity of the index by how well it predicts personal spiritual or paranormal experiences.

The remarkable difference between those scored high on the index and the others suggests that it will be quite adequate to only report the percent high in subsequent tables.

TABLE 55
New Age Index and Spiritual Experiences

	New Age Index			
	Zero	One	Two	High
Percent who have felt they were one with the universe	8%	13%	19%	51%
Percent who have felt they had left their bodies for a period of time	10%	9%	9%	41%

So, is New Age dominated by the highly educated? Yes. Only 8 percent of those who did not go beyond high school score high on the New Age Index, compared with 19 percent of those who attended college and 29 percent of those who went to graduate school. In contrast, the effect of income is inconsistent and tangled up with gender and region. For example, high-income people are far more likely to be into New Age than are low-income people if they live on the West Coast, but that is not true in the South where lower-income women are far more likely than wealthier women to score high on the New Age Index. The inconsistencies are partly produced by religious differences, as seen in Table 56.

TABLE 56
Denomination and the New Age Index

	Scored high
Unitarian	77%
United Church of Christ	18%
Episcopalian	23%
Methodist	16%
Presbyterian	17%
Lutheran	8%
All Liberal Protestants	*18%*
Pentecostal	13%
Baptist	7%
Assemblies of God	4%
All Conservative Protestants	*8%*
Latter-day Saints (Mormon)	3%
Roman Catholic	12%
Jewish	32%
No Religion	38%

This clearly fits the expected pattern. Persons identified with the more "liberal" denominations, or who claim "no religion," are far more likely to score high on the New Age Index than are those affiliated with more conservative groups or Roman Catholics. That a third of the Jews in our sample also score high reflects a quite well-known finding stemming from the high proportion of American Jews who are purely secular: converts to new religious groups—such as Hare Krishna, Scientology, or various forms of witchcraft—are overwhelmingly recruited from irreligious homes; hence, Jews are extremely overrepresented in these groups.[7]

Another way to see these religious effects is to examine the label that respondents said best described their religious identity.

TABLE 57
Religious Identification and New Age Index

	Percent high on index
Seeker	55%
Theological liberal	41%
Theological conservative	9%
Evangelical	14%
Bible-believing	11%
Born again	7%

More than half who identify themselves as seekers (55%) score high on the New Age Index, as did 41 percent of theological liberals. In contrast, very few theological conservatives, Evangelicals, Bible-believers, or the born again scored high.

New Age believers also are very inclined to have a vague conception of God.

TABLE 58
New Age Index and God

	New Age Index			
	Zero	One	Two	High
Percent who conceive of God as "a higher power or cosmic force"	6%	10%	15%	37%

Of course, factors besides education and religion influence responses to the New Age movement:

• *Gender*: Women (21%) are more likely than men (14%) to score high.

• *Region*: People on the West Coast (23%) are the most likely to score high, while people living in the Midwest (14%) are least likely.

• *Marital Status*: Unmarried couples living together are the most likely to score high (38%), followed by the never married (24%), the divorced (19%), married (15%), and widowed (12%).

• *Age*: Some of the marital effect is really related to age: those under age thirty are the most likely to score high (24%), and those over sixty are the least likely (12%).

• *Race*: Racial differences are insignificant.

• *Politics*: Strong Republicans are least apt to score high (11%), while strong Democrats are the most likely (23%). Only 10 percent who voted for Bush in 2004 score high, compared with 24 percent of those who voted for Kerry, and 33 percent of those who voted for Nader.

People who approve of marijuana are far more likely to score high (35%) than are people who completely disapprove (8%).

Finally, 31 percent of those who score high in the Index of Occult and Paranormal Belief also score high on the New Age Index, compared with 8 percent of those with low occult and paranormal scores.

CONCLUSION

As anticipated, the New Age movement is sustained by those highly educated Americans who lack an anchorage in conventional faith. This is consistent with the finding that converts to novel religions are overwhelmingly well educated and lacking a prior religious commitment—most were raised in irreligious or at least nonreligious homes. This also is consistent with the fact that New Age activities are clustered in very expensive resort communities such as Sedona, Arizona, and Big Sur and Ojai, California.

Contributors: Carson Mencken and Christopher Bader

17

THE IRRELIGIOUS
Simply Unchurched—Not Atheists

M uch is being made of an apparent rise in the percentage of Americans who report that they have no religious affiliation.[1] Recent surveys find that 11 to 12 percent now say they have no religion, while surveys conducted from the late 1940s through the 1980s found that only about 6 to 7 percent reported they had no religion.[2] It appears that after decades of stability, the number of respondents claiming "no religion" began to rise in the early 1990s.[3] This increase has been widely interpreted to mean that irreligion is increasing in America.

In both 2005 and 2007, the Baylor Surveys found 11 percent of the national sample reported they had "no religion." But are these people really irreligious?

Only about a third of the No Religion group are atheists who reject "anything beyond the physical world," while two-thirds of them expressed some belief in God. Thus, as reported in chapter 14, whatever increases may have taken place in the number of those without a religion offer no support for the assumption that atheism is increasing. Granted, many of these respondents are somewhat uncertain what they believe. Notice, however, that slightly more than a third confess their belief in a "higher power or cosmic force," which is the conception of "God" that is popular among adherents of New Age.

TABLE 59

"No Religion" and Belief in God

Which one statement comes closest to your personal beliefs about God?

	No religion
I have *no doubts* that God exists	11%
I believe in God, but with *some doubts*	6%
I *sometimes* believe in God	2%
I believe in a *higher power or cosmic force*	36%
I don't believe in anything beyond the physical world	31%
I have no opinion	14%
	100%

What else can be learned about the religiousness of these people? To pursue that question, in Table 60 the atheists were removed.

Even with the atheists omitted, belief in Jesus as the Son of God is unusual among persons claiming to have no religion (16%). However, one of four is willing to recognize him as a messenger or prophet from God, albeit only one of many.

Consistent with their response that they have no religion, these people seldom if ever attend church, which certainly makes sense (see Table 61). But the majority (56%) pray, and a third of them pray quite often. What then can they mean when they say they have no religion?

TABLE 60
"No Religion" and Belief in Jesus

Which one statement comes closest to your personal beliefs about Jesus?

	No religion (excluding atheists)
Jesus is the Son of God	16%
Jesus was one of many messengers or prophets of God	24%
Jesus was an extraordinary person, but he was not the Son of God	25%
Jesus probably existed, but he was not special	14%
Jesus is a fictional character	7%
I have no opinion	14%
	100%

TABLE 61
Religious Activity of Those Reporting "No Religion"

Ever attend church	20%
Ever pray	56%
Pray several times a week or more	32%

TABLE 62

Religious Beliefs of Those Reporting "No Religion"

In your opinion, does each of the following exist?	
Satan	33%
Hell	28%
Demons	37%
Heaven	42%
Angels	50%
Ghosts	46%

Around a third of these respondents profess belief in Satan, hell, and demons and around half of them believe in angels and ghosts. As with conceiving of God as a "higher power or cosmic force," and Jesus as one of many messengers from God, these findings suggest a strong element of New Age belief among those having "no religion."

TABLE 63

"No Religion" and Involvement in New Age

New Age Index	
High	50%
Medium	16%
Low	20%
Zero	14%
	100%

What "no religion" seems to mean to most who give this response is that they reject conventional religions, but not supernaturalism of more exotic sorts—two-thirds of them can be classified as New Agers.

TABLE **64**
"No Religion" and Belief in Bigfoot

Index of Occult and Paranormal Beliefs

High	39%
Medium High	23%
Medium	22%
Low	16%
	100%

Fully in keeping with their embracing New Age, those who say they have no religion also are very likely to accept occult and paranormal beliefs.

CONCLUSION

To sum up, most people who say they have no religion are not irreligious, but are unchurched. They certainly are not the hard-headed secularists that recent atheist writers make them out to be. To trade belief in Jesus for the Loch Ness Monster, Atlantis, and Bigfoot; to prefer astrology to the Bible; or to trade miracles for haunted houses and UFOs may be many things, but atheism they are not.

Some people who say they have no religion are atheists. But the far more interesting fact is that about two-thirds of such people are unchurched, not irreligious. They are unchurched, at least in part, because they hold religious notions that are not compatible with the organized faiths. But, of course, people typically drift into New Age beliefs because they are not participants in a religious community where such beliefs are ridiculed. It seems important that even though such people attend many public lectures, patronize New Age shops and bookstores, and many even join retreats in such fashionable alternative-religion centers as Sedona, Arizona, they persist in calling themselves "students" and "seekers" and never commit to any organized creed or group.[4] In that sense they are quite correct when they say they have no religion.

PART IV

THE PUBLIC SQUARE

FAITH AND POLITICS
Is There a Secret Plot of Evangelicals to Take Over the American Government?

Evangelical Christians are the new scapegoats of liberal American culture. A survey of a national sample of college professors conducted in 2006 found that 53 percent admitted to having negative feelings toward Evangelicals, compared with 3 percent having such feelings towards Jews and 18 percent toward atheists.[1] These findings are entirely consistent with a deluge of hysterical warnings against an impending theocracy and other calamities if something isn't done soon to curb these religious fanatics.

In his best-selling *American Theocracy*, Kevin Phillips identified President Bush as the "Theocrat-in-Chief," rambled on about "cultural anti-modernism," described the elections of 2000 and 2004 as caused by growing "disenlightenment," referred to Evangelicals as victims of "half baked preaching," and peppered the book with quotes denouncing Evangelicals, such as Harvey Cox's claim that evangelical religion is a "toxin endangering the health—even the life—of the Christian churches and American society."[2] This won Phillips fulsome praise in such publications as *Time* magazine and *The New York Times*.

In a blurb on the back cover of Michelle Goldberg's breathless revelations of a plot by Evangelicals to take over America, the angry atheist author Sam Harris wrote that Goldberg's

> *Kingdom Coming* reveals just how thoroughly our national discourse has been corrupted by the mad work of religious literalists. . . . Tens of millions of our neighbors are working each day to obliterate the separation of church and state, to supplant scientific rationality with Iron Age fantasies, and to achieve a Christian theocracy in the twenty-first century.[3]

Rabbi James Rudin began his revelation of *The Religious Right's Plans for the Rest of Us* this way:

> A Specter is haunting America. . . . It is the specter of Americans kneeling in submission to a particular interpretation of religion. . . . It is the specter of our nation ruled by the extreme Christian right, who would make the United States a "Christian nation" wherein their version of God's law supersedes all human law.[4]

It would be possible to quote briefly from other new, well-reviewed, and quite commercially successful books like these for many pages. Indeed, books warning about an evangelical Christian takeover are being published so frequently that they constitute a new literary genre. Unfortunately, even most of the far more temperate and informed commentators on the politics of evangelical Americans share with the extremists the belief that Evangelicals are very different from other Americans, that they are far more conservative politically, and that this conservatism is rooted in old-fashioned moral convictions on such matters as sexual norms and in right-wing views concerning economic issues such as welfare—but most of all that they are "extremists" in their opposition to the separation of church and state.

Given how often these issues are included in opinion polls, it is amazing that little or no data have been offered to support claims about the ideological chasms separating Evangelicals from everyone else. This chapter is intended to make up for that deficiency.

IDENTIFYING EVANGELICALS

Typically, Evangelicals have been identified on the basis of their denominational preference. Hence, Baptists, Nazarenes, Pentecostals, and members of other "conservative" denominations are classed as Evangelicals, while Presbyterians, Episcopalians, Methodists, and other religious "liberals" are excluded, and so are Roman Catholics. This is unsatisfactory on two counts. First, many members of the conservative denominations deny that they are Evangelicals, while many members of the more liberal denominations, and even some Roman Catholics, claim that they are. Overall, 28 percent of Americans embrace the label: Evangelical. This can be observed in Table 65.

TABLE 65
Denominational Group and Self-Identification as Evangelicals

	Describe themselves as "evangelical"
Conservative Protestants	49%
Liberal Protestants	28%
Roman Catholic	14%
Nondenominational Protestants	44%
No religion	2%
Total sample	28%

Clearly, to infer who is and who is not an Evangelical from their denominational preference is, at best, a rough measure and justified only when self-identification data are unavailable. Consequently, in this chapter, an evangelical Christian is someone who accepts that designation.

CHURCH AND STATE

The principle of the complete separation of church and state is, in fact, quite new, having first been asserted by the Supreme Court in 1947. Until then, the First Amendment was interpreted quite literally: "Congress shall make no law respecting the establishment of religion or prohibiting the free exercise thereof." That was long taken to mean that the government could not finance a religious organization or pass discriminatory laws against religious groups. Period. No one suggested that the government was required to be strictly secular. But then, in 1947, in the case of *Everson v. Board of Education*, the Supreme Court claimed that "The First Amendment has erected a wall between church and state. That wall must be kept high and impregnable. We could not approve the slightest breach."[5]

Subsequently, that ruling has been expanded and reinforced by decisions such as those that outlawed school prayers and the display of religious symbols on government property. Out went Christmas nativity scenes on public land; down went the Ten Commandments from schoolroom and courthouse walls. Soon it was illegal for school choirs to sing Christmas carols or for students eating in a school cafeteria to say grace out loud.[6]

Evangelical Christians are widely accused of wishing to reverse these rulings, and this is offered as evidence of their theocratic aims. Let's test this theory by analyzing the data in Table 66.

If one looked only at the third section of the table, one would agree that Evangelicals may pose a threat to the separation of church and state in that two-thirds of them do not support a strict separation of church and state while a slight majority of other Americans do. But that interpretation must change dramatically when one looks at the first two parts of the table. There we see that not only do most Evangelicals think it ought to be legal to display religious symbols in public spaces, but so does most everyone else. The same is true of school prayer. Yes, Evangelicals would restore that right, as would most Americans. What seems evident is that

---

TABLE 66
Separation of Church and State

Do you agree that the federal government *should*
1. "allow the display of religious symbols in public spaces"?

Evangelicals	88%
Liberal Protestants	72%
Roman Catholics	74%
No religion	26%
All non-Evangelicals	61%

2. "allow prayer in public schools"?

Evangelicals	94%
Liberal Protestants	67%
Roman Catholics	76%
No religion	21%
All non-Evangelicals	60%

3. "enforce a strict separation of church and state"?

Evangelicals	33%
Liberal Protestants	53%
Roman Catholics	54%
No religion	81%
All non-Evangelicals	58%

---

substantial numbers of non-Evangelicals don't really know what strict separation of church and state means these days—it is to them nothing but a slogan that they affirm in contradiction to their views on the two of the most visible applications of that slogan. In contrast, Evangelicals seem more aware of what is implied by the strict separation of church and state and therefore reject it.

The most important lesson to be drawn from Table 66 is that if a national referendum were held to restore school prayer and to allow religious symbols in public places, even if Evangelicals were prohibited from voting, the proposal would pass by a landslide. That does not mean, however, that Evangelicals fully reject the separation of church and state, as can be seen in Table 67.

TABLE 67
Federal Funding of Faith-based Organizations

---

*Do you agree that the federal government should
"fund faith-based organizations"?*

Evangelicals	44%
Liberal Protestants	26%
Roman Catholics	27%
No religion	7%
All non-Evangelicals	27%

It is true that Evangelicals are more likely than other Americans to support government funding for faith-based organizations, but the majority of them are opposed, as are the majority of Americans in general.

POLITICAL PREFERENCE AND PARTICIPATION

Evangelicals voted overwhelmingly for George W. Bush—76 percent of Evangelicals said he was the candidate they favored in the 2004 election. It also is true that the majority (58%) of Evangelicals are Republicans (only 20 percent said they were Democrats). However, as portrayed by the media, evangelical support goes far beyond their numbers at the voting booth—it is claimed that they are unusually active in political campaigning. In 2005, all respondents were asked if they had participated in activities concerning political activism in the year prior to the 2004 presidential election. The results are in Table 68.

So much for the media image of Evangelicals on the march. They were slightly less likely to make campaign contributions, significantly less likely to work in campaigns, and a bit less likely to attend meetings and rallies.

TABLE 68
Political Activism

"In the year leading up to the 2004 presidential election, did you":

	Make a campaign contribution	Work in a campaign	Attend a meeting
Evangelicals	27%	6%	15%
Liberal Protestants	32%	11%	21%
Roman Catholics	33%	11%	18%
No religion	37%	9%	25%
All non-Evangelicals	29%	10%	19%

Beyond party preferences and political activism lie current issues. Two primary clusters of issues divide the American public. One cluster consists of social and economic policies, such as the regulation of business or dealing with the environment. The second cluster consists of moral concerns such as capital punishment and abortion. Evangelicals often are attacked for their positions on central issues in each cluster.

SOCIAL AND ECONOMIC ISSUES

Four items assessed social and economic issues:

"To what extent do you agree that the federal government *should:*
- "Regulate business practices more closely,"
- "Distribute wealth more evenly,"
- "Do more to protect the environment,"
- "Spend more on the military."

TABLE 69
Social and Economic Issues

	Regulate business	Distribute wealth	Protect environ.	Spend on military
Evangelicals	60%	46%	76%	55%
Liberal Protestants	64%	52%	82%	51%
Roman Catholics	66%	54%	83%	53%
No religion	75%	70%	93%	27%
All non-Evangelicals	66%	59%	84%	47%

Reading down each column, the overall finding is that Evangelicals are pretty much like everyone else in terms of their social and economic outlook. Thus, most Americans support closer regulation of business, and so do most Evangelicals. A majority of Americans want the government to do more to distribute wealth more evenly, and almost half of Evangelicals agree. The overwhelming majority of Americans want more done to protect the environment, and so do 76 percent of Evangelicals. Americans are about evenly split on increased funding for the military, and so are Evangelicals.

MORAL ISSUES

These four items assess major moral issues that stimulate current political conflicts.

"To what extent do you agree that the federal government *should:*
- "Abolish the death penalty,"
- "Promote affirmative-action programs."

"How do you feel about
- "Abortion . . . when the woman does not want the child?"
- "Sexual relations . . . between two adults of the same sex?"

TABLE 70
Moral Issues

	Abolish death penalty	Promote aff. action	Abortion wrong	Same-sex sexuality wrong
Evangelicals	16%	34%	94%	91%
Liberal Protestants	20%	47%	60%	60%
Roman Catholics	18%	42%	75%	57%
No religion	34%	47%	24%	14%
All non-Evangelicals	20%	47%	63%	56%

Here, too, we see that Evangelicals aren't that different in comparison with other Americans, as opposed to comparison with the positions much favored by the media. Thus, only 16 percent of Evangelicals would repeal the death penalty, but only 20 percent of non-Evangelicals would repeal it. The majority of Evangelicals do not want the government promoting affirmative-action programs, but neither do most other Americans. It is true that Evangelicals are nearly unanimous in their opposition to abortion for women who don't want the child, but nearly two-thirds of non-Evangelicals express the same view. Finally, while Evangelicals overwhelmingly think sexual relations between adults of the same gender are wrong, the majority of Americans agree with them on this issue too.

CONCLUSION

In the 1940s and 1950s, there were many popular books and articles in magazines such as *The Nation*, that exposed the secret plans by the Pope and his minions to take over America and stamp out all traces of democratic rule. In his 1949 bestseller, *American Freedom and Catholic Power*, Paul Blanshard devoted many pages to details of the theocratic regime in store for America if the

Catholic threat were not headed off. He proposed that Protestant Americans organize "a resistance movement designed to prevent the [Catholic] hierarchy from imposing its social policies upon our schools, hospitals, government and family organization."[7]

Today, these anti-Catholic concerns seem ridiculous. Hopefully, the equally spurious claims about evangelical theocratic plots will also soon seem equally ridiculous. For the fact is that Evangelicals are not so very different after all.

19

MERRY CHRISTMAS, JESUS
It's Okay to Put Sacred Symbols in Public Space

Amazingly, opinion researchers have almost entirely ignored Christmas. The only previous poll finding related to this holiday found that 67 percent of Americans prefer that advertisers use "Merry Christmas" rather than "Happy Holidays." This poll, by the Rasmussen Report (November 2007), also found that 57 percent said they definitely planned to attend a special church service either on Christmas Eve or Christmas Day, and only 30 percent said they would not be doing so.

In planning the 2007 Baylor Survey, the decision was made to devote two items to Christmas. The first asked: "At what age did you stop believing in Santa Claus?" The second asked: "Do you regularly put up a Christmas tree during the holidays?"

SANTA CLAUS

Frankly, no one involved in planning the Baylor Surveys had the slightest idea how many Americans had ever believed in Santa Claus or at what age they learned the bitter truth. Certainly, no one anticipated that only 9 percent of Americans would report that they had never believed. But that's precisely how it turned out. In fact, most Americans (55%) believed until they were six or older:

"At what age did you stop believing in Santa Claus?"

I never believed in Santa	9%
About age 3	4%
About 4 or 5	32%
6 or older	55%
	100%

So who were the people who never believed in Santa?

• Some of them were atheists—20 percent of whom denied ever having believed in Santa.

• Some of them were Jews, 46 percent of whom said they had never believed in Santa Claus (but there were only twenty-nine Jews in the sample, so that statistic is somewhat unreliable).

• Among Christians there are no denominational effects and even 90 percent of those with "no religion" believed in Santa.

• *Gender*: Men and women were equally likely to have believed in Santa, but women were a bit more likely (61%) than men (49%) to have believed until they were six or older.

• *Region*: Apparently Santa gets to every part of the nation, as there are no significant regional effects.

• *Race*: There are no racial differences.

• *Marital Status*: Married or single, divorced or widowed, people are equally likely to have believed in Santa.

• *Politics*: Republicans and Democrats, liberals and conservatives, are all equally likely to have believed in Santa.

• *Education*: Education had no effect.

• Belief in Bigfoot, aliens, and ghosts is unrelated to belief in Santa.

• Not surprisingly, people who believed in Santa are much more likely to put up a Christmas tree regularly (89%) than those who never believed (64%).

CHRISTMAS TREES

Most Americans regularly put up a Christmas tree: 87 percent do so.

• Among Christians denomination had no effect and even 73 percent of those with "no religion" put up a tree. In fact, 68 percent of self-identified atheists also put up Christmas trees.

• In these data, only 14 percent of Jews reported that they regularly put up a tree. This is far below the 30 percent who put up trees according to the 1991 census of American Jews. Since that figure was based on thousands of Jewish respondents, we suspect that our results are too low and the result of the very small number of Jews in the sample.

• *Gender*: Women (90%) are a bit more likely than men (83%) to put up a tree regularly.

• *Marital Status*: Christmas trees are related to marital status: married people (91%) and people living together (90%) are more apt to put up a tree than are those who are still single (72%) and the divorced (79%).

• *Children*: People without children (74%) are less likely to put up a tree than are those with one child (88%) or those with two or more children (93%).

• *Region*: There are no regional differences.

• *Race*: There are no racial differences.

• *Age*: People of all ages are equally likely to put up a tree.

• *Politics*: Republicans (93%) are a bit more likely to put up trees than are Democrats (85%), and people who identify themselves as "extremely liberal" are substantially less likely than others to put up a tree (69%).

CONCLUSION

Although the data show that some kinds of people are a bit more likely than others to put up Christmas trees and to have believed in Santa Claus, the overwhelming finding is that, except for Jews, most Americans are into Christmas. Even most atheists put up trees and grew up believing in Santa. And that's probably why two-thirds of Americans agree that "The federal government should allow the display of religious symbols in public spaces."

20

INCIVILITY
Talking about Faith in Public

dvisors on proper etiquette used to suggest that in polite company one must never discuss politics or religion. Today, when polite company has gone the way of the formal dinner party, it is not clear that there are rules of etiquette, and, in any event, the advice to avoid talking about politics and religion seems long forgotten. But the point of that advice may well remain—that these topics raise matters of fundamental disagreement and can cause unpleasant exchanges and hurt feelings. On the other hand, that advice may no longer be pertinent. Perhaps new norms of religious civility make it possible to talk about religion without embarrassment or rancor.

These five items were included in the 2005 Baylor Survey to explore the social consequences of talking about religion.

How comfortable would you feel talking about religion with:

your family?

Not at all comfortable	4%
Somewhat uncomfortable	7%
Somewhat comfortable	24%
Very comfortable	65%
	100%

your friends?

Not at all comfortable	6%
Somewhat uncomfortable	8%
Somewhat comfortable	34%
Very comfortable	52%
	100%

your neighbors?

Not at all comfortable	13%
Somewhat uncomfortable	18%
Somewhat comfortable	36%
Very comfortable	33%
	100%

your co-workers?

Not at all comfortable	13%
Somewhat uncomfortable	18%
Somewhat comfortable	36%
Very comfortable	33%
	100%

strangers?

Not at all comfortable	23%
Somewhat uncomfortable	25%
Somewhat comfortable	30%
Very comfortable	22%
	100%

Most Americans are comfortable talking about religion with most people—only when it comes to strangers do nearly half say they would be uncomfortable. These results suggest that among people who know one another, there is a level of civility that makes it safe to discuss religion. Of course, the topic may be safe to talk about with friends and family, and even perhaps with neighbors, because there is so much agreement. But that would not seem to be so likely among co-workers (and, of course, the percent who would feel uncomfortable does rise on this item).

To pursue the matter further, the five items listed above were summed to create an Index of Anticipated Incivility, ranging from Zero (those who felt no discomfort in any situation) to High (those who were less than comfortable in all five).

TABLE 71
Religion and Index of Anticipated Incivility

	High	Zero
Conservative Protestants	10%	31%
Liberal Protestants	29%	15%
Catholics	29%	14%
Jews	27%	11%
Atheists	39%	12%
Latter-day Saints (Mormon)	11%	29%

By far, conservative Protestants and Mormons fear incivility the least, while atheists stand at the top—a third of atheists reported they would not feel comfortable talking about religion even with their families. That ought to surprise no one, since atheists can anticipate that nearly everyone will disagree with them (see chapter 14). By the same token, people who attend church more than once a week were the least apprehensive (3%) and those who never attend were the most (41%).

If disagreement, real or anticipated, is the basis for individuals' being reluctant to talk about religion, then people with irreligious friends ought to be especially likely to want to avoid the topic.

As is clear in Table 72, friendship is a major factor. People whose friends are irreligious are far more likely to not want to talk about religion.

TABLE 72
Irreligious Friends and Index of Anticipated Incivility

How many of your friends are not religious at all?			
Most	About half	A few	None

Incivility Index:				
High	40%	36%	17%	13%

As for other factors:

• *Gender*: Men (27%) are slightly, but statistically significantly, more likely than women (22%) to be reluctant to talk about religion.

• *Race*: Whites (26%) are far less willing than African Americans (7%) to talk to others about religion.

• *Politics*: Nader supporters (42%) were the most apprehensive about talking about religion, followed by Kerry voters (31%) and those who backed President Bush (19%).

• *Region*: People in the East (33%) were most apt to score high, and those in the South were least apt (17%).

• *Age*: There were no age differences.

• *Education*: Education made no difference either; those without any college (27%) were just like those who went to graduate school (27%),

CONCLUSION

In the days when it was thought impolite to discuss religion or politics in company, the concern was primarily over denominational disagreements. Today, it would appear that concern is focused on differences between the religious and the irreligious, with the latter being apprehensive about stirring up trouble.

RELIGIOUS-MEDIA CONSUMPTION
The *Da Vinci Code* Effect

In recent decades there has been a explosion of media religion in America—cable channels, network television series, movies, books, art, and recorded music with explicit religious content. Although media religion has generated a great deal of comment, it has prompted remarkably little market analysis. Who are the consumers? Is the audience limited to very religious people?

The Baylor Religion Survey included the first-ever extensive battery of religious-consumption items, which provided empirical evidence of this phenomenon. But more important, we have the first available data that allows us to see relationships between religious consumption and other aspects of religious life.

The Baylor Religion Survey asked respondents to report whether they had made any purchases in the last month from among each of thirteen different genres of goods. Of these, nine deal specifically with religious media: sacred texts, religious art, music, films, fiction, nonfiction, study materials, educational products, and devotional materials. Purchasing from a particular genre assumes that one consumes goods in that genre, and in this case such consumption refers to religious media specifically. We merged some of the above-mentioned items into three categories of religious-media consumption: reading materials, film, and music, and found that between one-fifth and two-fifths of our sample purchased goods from one of these genres. Using these measures, a little over half of the sample made purchases from any of these media genres. This suggests that religious consumption is a very important facet for many in the postindustrial age.

When we compare religious-media genre consumption along various religious characteristics, we find some expected and not-so-expected relationships. In terms of religious affiliation, evangelical Protestants stand apart from Catholics, mainline Protestants, and the nonaffiliated with the highest average amount of religious consumption overall (64%), religious film and music purchases (31% and 37% respectively), and book purchases (53%).[1] Mainline Protestants are a distant second in most cases, and even fewer Catholics reported consuming religious goods. But perhaps most striking are the results of the nonaffiliated. About 20 percent of those who claim no religious affiliation consumed at least one of the three types of religious media, and most often these were religious book purchases (12%).

But not all religious individuals necessarily identify with a religious tradition. One could attend church quite regularly and not consider oneself an Evangelical or Episcopalian. When we analyzed church attendance, we found that the most devout were clearly more likely to consume these religious-media goods. About 78 percent of those who attended church "several times a week" had made a recent religious-media purchase, compared to 43 percent of those who attended less than once a month. This pattern is repeated when we analyzed each of the main types of religious-media genres. While a minority of the most devout purchased a religious video (38%), all other groups had even lower proportions on this item. As with nonaffiliation, we paid close attention to the nonattenders, and again we were surprised to see that 20 percent of those who never attend church made a religious-media purchase, and most of this fell under the religious book category (13%).

TABLE 73

Consumption of Religious Media by Genre and Church Attendance

Attendance Group	1+ Products (any type)	1+ Books	1+ Music products	1+ Videos
All respondents	51%	42%	23%	22%
Never	20%	13%	5%	6%
Less than once per month	43%	31%	10%	21%
1–3 times per month	57%	46%	27%	23%
About weekly	71%	64%	36%	28%
Several times per week	78%	68%	58%	38%

While affiliation and behavior are helpful indicators of individual religiosity, most religious practitioners would argue that one's beliefs indicate a great deal about one's actual faith. In this respect we looked at how respondents viewed the Bible to get a sense of how religious consumption might be associated with one kind of belief. Without question, those who believe the Bible is the literal "word of God" made religious media purchases far and above those with any other view of the Bible. About 71 percent of biblical literalists made a religious-media purchase, and again the specific genre most often purchased was religious reading material. Of particular note, again we found that the most unorthodox were not necessarily absent from religious consumer purchases. A full 27 percent of those who viewed the Bible as an "ancient book of history and legends" made at least one religious media purchase, and again it was religious reading materials that took the largest share here.

THE DA VINCI DIFFERENCE

Not all religious media are the same, however. It has been pointed out that there are significant distinctions in religious-media consumption in the United States.[2] Catholics and Evangelicals, for example, more often watched *The Passion of the Christ*, as opposed to reading *The Da Vinci Code*. The Baylor Religion Survey again proves useful in exploring these nuances. Respondents were not only asked whether they had made purchases of religious goods in these genres, but also whether they had read particular best sellers and seen specific contemporary television and film examples. In our analysis we included readership on the following items: the Left Behind series, *The Purpose-Driven Life*, *The Da Vinci Code*, *The Celestine Prophecy*, any book by noted Evangelical James Dobson, and any book in the Dianetics series. We applied the same measures of religiosity for genre consumption here and found that specific examples of religious reading material have different audiences. In some ways this was not altogether surprising. Evangelicals, for example, were far more likely to have read the Left Behind series (33%), *The Purpose-Driven Life* (31%), and books by James Dobson (34%), but we were somewhat surprised by how low these results were given that over 50 percent of evangelical Protestants purchased religious-themed reading material in the past year. Mainline Protestants, Catholics, and the nonaffiliated progressively showed much lower proportions of their constituents reading these particular books. When we consider the other religiously themed books, however, we find that few respondents reported reading best-sellers such as *The Celestine Prophecy* and *Dianetics*; indeed the largest readership among these groups was the nonaffiliated, where less than 12 percent of whom reported reading *The Celestine Prophecy*. But most striking was the readership for *The Da Vinci Code*. About one-third of mainline Protestants, Catholics, and the nonaffiliated reported reading this work, but another 18 percent of Evangelicals did as well. The controversy over the portrayal of the Catholic Church notwithstanding, this work of fiction has surprisingly crossed religious lines where other best-sellers could not.

When we compared church attendance rates and readership of these works, we found strikingly similar patterns to the religious-affiliation findings if one associated greater religious piety with Evangelicalism. Indeed, larger proportions of the most religiously active were reading the evangelical titles; 44 and 42 percent of those who attend church several times a week reported reading *The Purpose-Driven Life* and works by James Dobson. At the same time very few of those who do not attend church read these types of religious works (1% and 2% respectively). The nontraditional religious works had similar patterns to religious affiliation as well; no more than 10 percent of any level of church attendance reported reading *The Celestine Prophecy* or any book in the Dianetics series. And again *The Da Vinci Code* stands apart as a unique work that garnered a sizeable minority of nearly every church attender (and nonattender). A full 33 percent of those who never attend church read this work, and even 13 percent of those who attend church several times a week reported the same.

Perhaps most illustrative of the different measures of religiosity and consumption of specific religious works was views of the Bible. As with church attendance and religious affiliation, the more orthodox or conservative in their view of the Bible were more likely to report reading the evangelical titles. A full 34–35 percent of those who believe the Bible to be the literal word of God had read the Left Behind series, *The Purpose-Driven Life*, and any book by Dobson. Less than 8 percent of those who viewed the Bible as an "ancient book of history and legends" had read any of these titles. In similar fashion to the other measures of religiosity, fairly low proportions of those with any view of the Bible reported reading the two non-Christian religious best-sellers; only 12 percent of those who view the Bible as ancient history had read *The Celestine Prophecy* and another 10 percent reported reading *Dianetics*. Finally, *The Da Vinci Code* again garnered a sizeable readership regardless of one's view of the Bible. Nearly half of those who viewed the Bible as ancient history or "containing human error" (46% and 45% respectively) had read this work. And while only a minority of biblical literalists had read *The Da Vinci Code*, they had the largest readership of non-Christian works, as seen in Table 74.

TABLE 74

Reading of Popular Religious or Spiritual Book Titles

[Percentage within each group]

View of the Bible	Left Behind	Purpose	Dobson	Da Vinci	Celestine	Dianetics
All respondents	20%	20%	18 %	30%	7%	5%
Ancient book of history and legends	7%	5%	3%	46%	12%	10%
Some human error	15%	10%	5%	45%	9%	5%
True but not literal	22%	22%	22%	27%	6%	4%
Literal, word for word	34%	34%	35%	12%	3%	1%

ANGELIC AIRWAVES

In addition to the specific book titles, we also asked respondents whether they had seen a variety of specific visual popular religious media, including: *Touched by an Angel, Joan of Arcadia, 7th Heaven,* Benny Hinn's *This Is Your Day, The Passion of the Christ,* and the VeggieTales franchise. Generally we found that larger shares of various religious groups and degrees of religiosity reported watching these items. This may not be all that surprising given that much less effort is required to watch than read media. With that in mind, we found larger shares (and majority shares in some instances) of the most devout and orthodox reporting the viewing of specific religious media. In terms of church attendance, for example, the most frequent attenders ("several times a week") more often watched *The Passion of the Christ,* VeggieTales, Benny Hinn, and *Touched by an Angel* compared to any other type of church attender. Biblical literalists and evangelical Protestants also stood apart from others in this respect. In one particular instance, however, we were surprised at how many religious Americans resonated with the highly rated television series *Touched by an Angel.* More than half of every level of religiosity and orthodoxy (except for the least observant) reported watching this show. Additionally, the majority of mainline Protestants and Catholics viewed this program (57% and 60% respectively). But much like other types of religious media, we also found that sizeable minorities of the least observant and nonaffiliated watched religiously themed visual media. Between 25 and 29 percent of those who view the Bible as an "ancient book of history and legends" had watched *The Passion of the Christ, Joan of Arcadia,* and *7th Heaven,* and over 37 percent of them reported watching *Touched by an Angel.* Similarly, proportions of those who report never attending church viewed these items, and again *Touched by an Angel* took the largest viewership among the nonattending. Finally, we found that a significant minority among the nonaffiliated reported viewing these media items as well: nearly 20 percent of the nonaffiliated reported watching *The*

TABLE 75

Viewing of Popular Religious or Spiritual Programs, Films, or Video Products
[Percentage within each tradition]

	Passion	VeggieTales	7th Heaven	Touched	Joan	B. Hinn
All respondents	44%	25%	41%	58%	30%	7%
Evangelical Protestant	60%	39%	52%	66%	32%	11%
Mainline Protestant	38%	23%	36%	57%	32%	4%
Catholic	45%	18%	38%	60%	30%	3%
Nonaffiliated	19%	9%	31%	33%	25%	2%

Passion of the Christ, another 25 percent had seen *Joan of Arcadia*, and about one-third had viewed *7th Heaven* and *Touched by an Angel*, as seen in the Table 75.

CONCLUSION

Highly religious and religiously conservative Americans tend to consume more religious media than most other Americans. However, religious groups tend to consume goods that are more in alignment with their core beliefs, but in some cases, certain religious media have had a strong crossover among different religious audiences. In our examples *The Da Vinci Code* and *Touched by an Angel* picked up larger shares of audiences that normally do not identify with the themes of these media examples. More broadly we also noted that the least observant and least orthodox were not absent from consuming religious goods. This suggests that indeed consumer behavior may be a unique postmodern means by which many Americans who are not religious by traditional standards actually gain exposure to religious themes, concepts, and narratives.

Contributors: Jerry Z. Park and Scott Draper

22

CIVIC PARTICIPATION
Faith as Social Capital

Social critics have frequently charged that Americans lack civic engagement and that what little there is has been declining—that Americans are increasingly dropping out of group activities, whether they be social clubs or community-service organizations.

Robert Bellah and his covey of coauthors described the excesses of individualism and lack of civic engagement in their influential *Habits of the Heart* (1985). According to Bellah and his collaborators, many societal ills result from too great an emphasis on individualism and too weak a commitment to the community. Individualism harms the individual because only community participation can reduce alienation and "enable people to belong and contribute to the larger society."[1] Individualism harms society because it deprives the community of needed resources. However, despite the fact that all of the authors claim to be sociologists, and despite claiming to be based on several hundred personal interviews, the generalizations made in *Habits of the Heart* are asserted without reference to any statistics.

More than a decade after *Habits of the Heart*, Robert Putnam[2] agreed with Bellah and his colleagues, noting ominously that more Americans are "bowling alone." Putnam exploited this remarkably evocative phrase as an indicator of the decline in civic engagement. On behalf of his thesis that we are becoming a nation of selflish loners, Putnam statistically documented the decline of many groups, including fraternal lodges such as the Eagles, Elks, and Masons and service clubs such as Rotary. He also claimed that Americans have become much less apt to take an active part in local political parties and organizations. And as noted in the introduction, Putnam also wrongly claimed that church attendance has long been in decline. Even if he was right about the decline of once-popular activities such as bowling leagues and fraternal lodges, Putnam failed to pay any attention to new activities such as the explosion of bicycle-riding clubs, environmental groups, or the deep involvement of millions in online groups and campaigns.

Robert Wuthnow provided a more nuanced version of Putnam's thesis in his book *Loose Connections*.[3] Wuthnow conceded that many civic activities cited by Putnam may not be declining but argued that this is misleading because the participants are no longer as committed to these activities as they once were. In addition, Wuthnow claimed to detect a shift from some traditional organizations such as religious denominations to new, less demanding types of groups such as nondenominational churches, megachurches, and a "new spirituality." Thus, he argued that denominationalism has become less significant and claimed that "since World War II an increasing role has been played by other kinds of organizational forms that function in ways different from those comprising the official hierarchies of denominations." According to Wuthnow, people now construct a "patchwork religion," taking particular beliefs from different religious traditions, and piecing together a new type of religious belief that is more compatible with their own values and a new type of religious organization requiring less involvement.

Previous chapters have contradicted many of Wuthnow's claims. Chapter 1 showed that denominationalism is thriving. chapters 2 and 3 showed that the more traditional and demanding denominations are growing rapidly, while the more tepid churches rapidly decline. Chapter 5 demonstrated that, if anything, the megachurch generates greater commitment and participation than do the small congregations whose decline Wuthnow laments. Chapter 17 revealed that the new "spirituality" without religion is not widespread and is not really irreligious.

Although the Baylor Survey of 2005 asked many questions about civic participation, it cannot provide data directly relevant to whether or not civic participation is declining, holding steady, or even, as Christopher Jencks[4] has claimed, on the rise. What these materials can provide is solid information on the current extent of many forms of participation to serve as benchmarks for future studies and allow insight into what factors may contribute to such participation at the present time.

Respondents to the 2005 Baylor Survey were asked to report their participation in these fifteen kinds of organizations, ordered here by the percent who claimed to belong to each kind.

Church or other religious organization	54%
Charitable organization	49%
Elementary, middle, or high school	31%
Sports, hobby, or leisure club/group	28%
Arts/cultural organization	28%
Political party, club, or association	26%
Civic or service group	22%
Trade union or professional association	22%
Neighborhood group or association	21%
Other group/organization	20%
School fraternities, sororities, or alumni association	18%
Youth groups or organizations	14%
Internet-based club, group, or chat room	12%
Therapeutic or counseling group	7%
Ethnic or racial organization	5%

Despite the fact that "church or other religious organization" is the most chosen type, most respondents seem to not have been reporting simple membership in a church (since 69 percent belong to a congregation) but to have properly interpreted the question as asking about church-connected organizations. In any event, the overall results suggest that levels of civic participation are quite high. This is further emphasized when these answers were added for each respondent.

Total Number of Organizations Belonged To:

None	31%
One	23%
Two	17%
Three	11%
Four	7%
Five	4%
Six	3%
Seven	2%
Eight or more	2%
	100%

A simple Index of Civic Participation (Table 76) was created by collapsing these answers into four categories: (1) zero, (2) one or two, (3) three or four, and (4) five or higher. The validity of this index can be demonstrated by using it to predict other forms of civic participation. Clearly the Index is tapping what it is meant to tap: the extent to which people participate in their communities.

We may now examine what sorts of people are more or less active participants.

• *Gender*: Contrary to what many would expect, women are not more active than men: 10 percent of men and 9 percent of women scored five or more.

• *Race*: African Americans and whites are equally likely to participate.

• *Income*: Lower income people are significantly less likely than upper-income people to participate.

• *Education*: People with less education are far less likely than the most educated to participate; 23 percent of those who have

TABLE 76
Index of Civic Participation and Other Aspects of Participation

In connection with the 2004 election, did you:

Civic Participation Index	zero	1–2	3–4	5 or more
Write, call, or visit a public official?	18%	25%	38%	51%
Give money to a political campaign, party, or candidate?	19%	26%	35%	53%
Visit internet sites related to the election?	34%	43%	51%	62%
Work for a political campaign or voter registration drive?	6%	6%	14%	29%
Do community volunteer work?	32%	42%	55%	72%

attended graduate school participate in five or more organizations compared with none of those who failed to complete high school.

• *Age*: Young and old are equally likely to participate in civic organizations.

• *Politics*: Bush and Kerry voters are equally likely to be active, but 63 percent of Nader voters participate in *no* organizations.

• *Religion*: The more often you attend church, the more likely you are to be active in civic organizations. However, people who belong to conservative Protestant denominations are significantly less likely to be active than are liberal Protestants and Roman Catholics, while Jews are substantially more likely to be active than are members of any other denominations. Atheists are less likely to be active than are members of any religious group.

CONCLUSION

Those who mourn the decline of the lodges, bowling teams, the League of Women Voters, and neighborhood political clubs may be correct as to these downward trends, but they seem unaware that even at their height, only a small percentage of Americans were involved in any of these groups. Compare this with the finding above that more than two-thirds of American adults actually belong to at least one of the organizations included in the Index of Civic Participation and that almost half belong to two or more. But, of course, it is very hard to get headlines from good news.

Contributors: Robyn Driskell and Larry Lyon

23

Going to College, Getting a Job
What Happens When Mom and Dad Take Their
Kids to Church

The introduction rejected the current anxieties that the churches are losing their young people by showing that young adults have been prone to nonattendance for as long as there have been polls on religious activity. It was suggested that many people let their religious participation lapse while they are single but most of them return to regular church attendance after they marry, and especially after they have children. That certainly was the case during the early 1960s as shown by the *American Piety* surveys. But it has been several decades since anyone has bothered to examine this pattern again. Is it still true?

Using data from two waves of the Baylor Survey (spring of 2005 and fall of 2006), we found the following:

• The average mother is 21 percent more likely to attend religious services at least twice a month, compared to a similar woman who doesn't have children;

• Even a parent (male or female) who is lacking in religious beliefs is about 50 percent more likely to attend religious services twice a month or more, compared to a similar person without children.

At a minimum, parents are a lot more likely to go to church than are people with no children.

The immediate effects of parents' taking kids to church can be quite dramatic; a recent study found that children from more religious families and from families with higher rates of religious attendance are better behaved and more well adjusted at home and at school.[1] This is true so long as there is no significant conflict over religion in the family.

Does this church-going behavior have any lasting beneficial impact in adulthood, over and above the benefits in childhood? The Baylor Surveys say that it does. Table 77 shows that better-educated people generally had parents who attended church services twice a month or more. Among people with at least some graduate-level education, two-thirds had mothers who were frequent church attenders, compared to just under half of people with only a high-school diploma. The difference is just as large when looking at frequent attendance by both parents and even larger when looking at fathers' attendance. This finding is consis-

TABLE 77
Parents' Religious Attendance and Education

Education level	Mother attended often*	Father attended often	Both parents attended often
Less than High-school graduate	49%	40%	38%
High-school graduate	49%	35%	34%
Some college	56%	37%	36%
Trade/technical training	59%	49%	46%
College graduate	65%	48%	45%
Postgraduate work or degree	66%	56%	51%

* "Often" is defined as attending religious services two times a month or more.

tent with recent research showing that church attendance during adolescence helps to mitigate a number of the harmful long-term effects of a disadvantaged childhood and leads to better educational outcomes across the board.[2]

There are a number of reasons why parents' religious attendance might improve children's educational and developmental outcomes. First, children may be more likely to learn good values and morals if they go to church. Second, a religious congregation can provide an important sense of community that can help develop social capital, interpersonal skills, and a sense of self-worth. Third, having parents who attend church together can help assure that a child grows up in an intact family. Consider the following statistics from the Baylor Surveys:

- The average person is 50 percent less likely to be divorced or separated if he or she attends religious services at least twice a month.
- The divorce rate among those who never attend religious services is close to double that of weekly church-goers.

If the parents are going to church—especially if they are going together—it is much more likely that the child had both parents living at home. And having an intact family has numerous benefits, both monetary and psychological: higher household income, better health care, more attention from parents, result in children who are less likely to smoke, less likely to have sex early, and more likely to be generally happy.[3] Any of these benefits could explain why children are more likely to get a good education when their parents attend church often.

Of course, the jobs that people do depend substantially on the amount of education they have. Since parental religious attendance affects educational outcomes, it should also affect people's occupational choices. The fall 2006 wave of the Baylor Survey asked about each respondent's job, including a general occupational classification. There were twenty-four different classifications, and we calculated the average educational attainment for each of the

twenty-four groups. We then sorted the occupations from highest
to lowest average education level and split the groups into three
categories of eight occupation groups—high education, mid-range
education, and low education.[4] Table 78 shows that the occupational groups differ as would be expected in terms of education.
The bottom two lines in the table reveal several very interesting
things. Among people with children, the more educated their occupational group, the higher their level of church attendance. But
among the childless, there is a weak relationship in the opposite
direction—the less-educated group is slightly more likely to attend
church at least twice a month. But perhaps of even greater inter-
est is that people in high- and mid-range-education occupations
dramatically increase their religious attendance when they have
children—while those in the less-educated occupations do not.

But we next asked whether the effects of parents' religious
habits on children's education are the same for both sexes. The

TABLE 78

Religious Attendance and Choice of Occupation

	High-education occupations	Mid-range-education occupations	Low-education occupations
Average years of schooling	15.4	13.4	12.7
Percent completing college	57.1%	15.0%	8.0%
Percent with children and currently attend at least twice a month	52.4%	48.0%	38.2%
Percent with no children and currently attend at least twice a month	26.0%	26.4%	32.3%

data shown in Tables 79 and 80 show that they are not. Parents' religious attendance has a much bigger impact on women's education than on men's. For men, there is no consistent relationship between either parent's church attendance and the amount of education ultimately achieved. For women, there is a positive relationship, at least up to the point of attending "about weekly." At the same time, this benefit is not the same at all levels of parents' attendance. There seems to be a drop-off effect, as if regular religious attendance is good for children, but it may be possible to have too much of a good thing.

TABLE 79

Mother's Religious Attendance and Child's Education by Gender

	Men		Women	
	Years of schooling	College completion rate	Years of schooling	College completion rate
Never	13.9	24.4%	13.7	19.6%
Less than once a year	13.7	13.8%	12.9	18.7%
Once or twice a year	14.9	54.5%	13.8	24.2%
Several times a year	14.1	30.2%	13.8	26.4%
Once a month	13.2	10%	14.2	31.8%
2–3 times a month	14.6	46.5%	14.7	42.2%
About weekly	14	25.4%	14.5	39.5%
Weekly	14.3	33.9%	14.2	30.1%
Several times a week	14.1	35.8%	13.9	26.6%

TABLE 80

Father's Religious Attendance and Child's Education by Gender

	Men		Women	
	Years of schooling	College completion rate	Years of schooling	College completion rate
Never	13.8	22.7%	13.6	18.4%
Less than once a year	14.3	28.5%	13.3	19%
Once or twice a year	14.9	55.7%	14.6	41.9%
Several times a year	13.9	24.9%	14.3	33.3%
Once a month	14.2	36.6%	14.1	33%
2–3 times a month	14.9	54%	15.4	53.7%
About weekly	14.2	24.6%	14.9	46.5%
Weekly	14.2	34.4%	14.1	31%
Several times a week	14	27.3%	14.2	32.1%

There are a number of reasons why we might see this starkly different impact of parental religious attendance on boys compared to girls. Perhaps girls are more inclined to benefit from the community that a church, synagogue, mosque, or temple provides. Perhaps church participation helps "keep them out of trouble." Or perhaps boys are so strongly impacted by other factors that determine their educational attainment that parents' religious attendance does not make a difference.

CONCLUSION

Feminists and other critics often accuse religion of being oppressive toward women, even of brainwashing women into accepting diminished roles in the home. In the United States, the phrase "barefoot and pregnant" is bandied about, and Kaiser Wilhelm II is attributed with coining "Kinder, Küche, Kirche" (children, kitchen, church) as a nineteenty-century ideal. The Baylor Survey tells us instead that religion in the United States has positive effects. When Mom and Dad go to church and take their kids with them, the kids get more education, especially the daughters. Taking the kids to church also provides a key to high-education jobs. Far from putting them in the kitchen against their wills, as critics might say, when Mom and Dad take daughters to church, they open up the future for them.

Contributors: Wafa Hakim Orman,
Charles M. North, and Carl R. Gwin

EPILOGUE
Institute for Studies of Religion (ISR) at Baylor

B
ecause Baylor University has long competed in major college sports and is a member of the powerful Big 12 Conference, few people realize that until quite recently it was primarily a fine undergraduate school. Serious efforts to add a distinguished research and graduate-school component began only several years ago. From the start it was recognized that as a Christian school, Baylor has superior resources to draw upon to quickly build programs and institutions devoted to research on religion. This emphasis has produced rapid results, most of them under the auspices of the Institute for Studies of Religion. This final chapter offers a summary of these recent developments.

In the spring of 2004, Baylor initiated an institute to foster research on religion and recruited Byron Johnson from the University of Pennsylvania and Rodney Stark from the University of Washington to serve as codirectors. For the first year, Johnson and Stark shared a small office, and their secretary had a windowless room across the hall. There was no funding. Four years later, the Institute has raised more than $8,000,000 in research grants, has an administrative staff of eleven, five resident postdoctoral fellows, substantial additional funding from the university and is engaged in the following major research initiatives.

The China Initiative

Beginning with a three-year grant from the John Templeton Foundation of $1,730,000, this project is training Chinese scholars how to do empirical social research with an emphasis on values and spirituality. At present three scholars from China are residents at Baylor as part of this program; workshops on research methods are being held in China and at Baylor; support is available for small-scale research projects in China; an institute devoted to research on religion has been established at Beijing University in close collaboration with Baylor's ISR; and access has been purchased to data from a survey of a national sample of Chinese adults (7,500 interviews) conducted by Horizon Research Consultancy Group Ltd, a Chinese polling firm. In addition, an online journal supported by ISR is being created to publish research by Chinese scholars in Chinese.

Dr. Carson Mencken, professor of sociology at Baylor, is directing the China Initiative (he also serves as the director of research for ISR). Mencken is assisted on the China Initiative by Fengang Yang of Purdue University, Anna Xiao Dong Sun of Kenyon College, and Yunfeng Lu, ISR's first postdoctoral fellow and now an assistant professor of sociology at Beijing University.

Initiative on Prosocial Behavior

Many scholars associated with ISR, including Johnson, Stark, Christopher Bader, and Sung Joon Jang, have done work in criminology, the social-science specialty devoted to asking why people commit criminal and deviant acts. All four of these scholars often felt that this focus was too narrow, and so they decided to stand the field of criminology on its head. At best, criminology only asks why some people don't commit crimes, but no one has been asking what makes people do "good" things. Not merely why don't some people break into homes, but why do some people return lost wallets? Why do they give to charities? Why do they volunteer to serve as "Big Brothers" or "Big Sisters"? Particular attention will be given to the effects of religion on prosocial behavior. This initiative has begun with a grant of $400,000 from the Office of Juvenile Justice and Delinquency Prevention of the United States Department of Justice. This project will culminate in a series of publications that examine the role of religion in self-control and reform as well as several studies using longitudinal data to determine the cumulative effect of adolescent religious involvement as a protective factor.

THE BAYLOR RELIGION SURVEYS

ISR will conduct a major survey of American religion every two years through 2018. The first was conducted in 2005 and the second in 2007, with the field work being done by the Gallup Organization and paid for by a grant of $716,000 from the John Templeton Foundation. Subsequently, Baylor University has agreed to fund five additional waves. Unlike the first two waves, these future surveys may not be based on a national sample of the entire U.S. population. Consideration is being given to devoting the 2009 study to a survey of a large sample of American Protestant congregations, allowing study of why some grow and others decline. Some thought is being given to limiting the 2011 survey to a national sample of Hispanics.

Christopher Bader, associate professor of sociology, was recently named director of the Baylor Surveys. In collaboration with Paul Froese, assistant professor of sociology, Bader is completing a book on American images of God—a study that began with the chapter included in this volume. This work is funded by a two-year grant of $256,000 from the John Templeton Foundation to support in-depth interviewing of many Americans about their conceptions of God.

INITIATIVE ON FAITH-BASED COMMUNITY PROJECTS

Many social problems fester for lack of human resources. The government can't afford to provide an individual parole officer for every newly released prisoner, nor can it provide immediate responses to rising family tensions. But there are millions of willing volunteers in American churches who could fill the gap if adequate organizations existed to place them where they are needed. The government has been experimenting with funding some of the needed coordination, but more importantly with providing research support to evaluate various programs. That is where ISR comes in.

The Faith and Community Technical Support (FACTS), a one-year pilot project of approximately $3,000,000 was awarded to ISR by the Office on Violence Against Women of the United States Department of Justice. ISR served as an intermediary between the federal government and small faith- and community-based organizations providing social services to victims of domestic violence in rural communities. These small faith- and community-based organizations were able to build organizational capacity, expand the involvement of volunteers, especially from religious congregations, and significantly expand services to victims of family violence.

The role of faith-based intermediaries is a grossly underdeveloped area and one that has considerable implications for many relevant public-policy issues from prisoner reentry to literacy, from mentoring to job training. In a era of evidenced-based government, where policymakers are requiring rigorous evaluation of programs, coupled with finite resources, ISR research is helping both faith-based practitioners and the federal government rethink how they may work together through intermediary organizations.

INITIATIVE ON THE ECONOMICS OF RELIGION

There is a huge literature proposing that economic development, especially the rise of capitalism, is closely linked to religion. But there has been an amazing lack of research to see if the economic behavior of individuals is related to their religious commitments. Hence, scholars at Baylor, especially Charles North, arranged to have a national sample of Americans polled by the Gallup Organization in 2007 about their economic and religious situations and beliefs. Although chapters 12 and 23 are based on this survey, serious analysis has just begun. Some studies also will be conducted at the level of nations to see how religion may be related to economic growth—and some studies will focus on historical cases. In addition, several workshops will be held to assist graduate students from across the nation conduct studies of religion and economics. This initiative is supported by a grant of $378,000 from the John Templeton Foundation.

INITIATIVES IN FORMATION

The following initiatives are in the exploratory and/or planning stage and may or may not be undertaken.

Initiative on Religious Tolerance

Perhaps no society in history has sustained such a degree of religious diversity as does contemporary America. Yet there has been very little actual research on the extent of intolerance among these many faiths. The lack of research takes on even greater significance because of the many signs that religious intolerance has been undergoing fundamental changes and becoming increasingly politicized. But little or no research has ever been devoted to prejudice against Catholics, various Protestant groups, Mormons, atheists, or the various brands of "new" spirituality, let alone studies of how these groups regard one another. For all these reasons, it is past time to take a careful look at the current anatomy of American religious intolerance. We are now seeking to fund this initiative in collaboration with the Institute of Jewish and Community Research (see below).

Initiative on Islam

This initiative may have two aspects. One involves surveys of Muslim societies. A preliminary step was taken during 2007 when

Alessandra Gonzalez, a Ph.D. student in the Baylor Department of Sociology and an ISR student fellow conducted a survey of a thousand college students in Kuwait about their religious and social attitudes, especially sex-role attitudes. Monsoor Moaddel, a distinguished Islamic scholar and a nonresident fellow of ISR, would play a leading role in this initiative. A second aspect of the initiative involves historical research on Muslim-Christian relations. In this regard, Rodney Stark is completing a book on the Crusades.

Interdisciplinary Journal of Research on Religion (IJRR)

During the first several months that ISR existed, plans were made to launch an online journal to publish the best research on religion. The mandate was broad: to include research from all of the social-science discipline, hence historical studies of the early church have appeared alongside quantitative studies of contemporary religious behavior. To attract attention and distinguish IJRR from other academic publications, authors are paid $1,000 for an article.

The first articles appeared in 2005 and clearly met expectations that high quality could be achieved from the start. Rodney Stark served as the founding editor of IJRR and William Swatos Jr. is the managing editor. Swatos also serves as the executive secretary of two leading scholarly organizations: the Religious Research Association and the Association for the Sociology of Religion. Expenses involved in the journal have been met by grants from the Stark/Roberts Foundation. Visit: www.religjournal.com.

Affiliated Institutes

ISR is involved in joint projects with three other research organizations.

The Institute of Jewish and Community Research (IJCR) in San Francisco has been conducting studies of religious tolerance for the past several years. ISR joined them in a recent survey of

American college professors, assessing their feelings toward various religious groups, including evangelical Christians, Mormons, Jews, Muslims, and atheists, as well as attitudes toward the state of Israel. Now ISR and IJCR are seeking funds to conduct a large national survey on these topics as noted above.

The Association of Religion Data Archives (ARDA) has been collecting data sets involving American religion since it was founded by Roger Finke in 1998. For example, ARDA has a large number of national and regional surveys devoted primarily to religion— including the 1963 church-member sample from the original *American Piety* study as well as the first Baylor Religion Survey done in 2005. In this way these studies remain available to future researchers, especially those wishing to examine historical trends. At present, ARDA is housed at Pennsylvania State University but has close ties to ISR.

The Center for Studies of Religion and Society at Beijing University was initiated in early 2008 and is modeled on ISR. Close cooperation between the two institutes is anticipated. Indeed, ISR and the Center on Religion and Chinese Society at Purdue University will stage an important conference in China (October 2008): "The Beijing Summit on Chinese Spirituality and Society" at Beijing University. The conference will bring together top scholars from China and around the world to present research on the social-scientific study of religion.

NONRESIDENT ISR FELLOWS

ISR has more than fifty prominent, nonresident fellows scattered around the world. These scholars often serve as consultants to and evaluators of ISR projects. Several joint ventures involving some of these scholars are in the planning stages.

CONCLUSION

In addition to all of this, there is a great deal of religious research going on in various Baylor departments. For example, sociology has initiated a Ph.D. in the sociology of religion, and seven members of the department specialize in doing research on religion. Several members of the history department recently have won prizes for their studies of religion, and there are fine scholars doing research on religion in the psychology, classics, economics, philosophy, and religion departments. For someone interested in religious research, Baylor is the place to be.

Contributors: Rodney Stark and Byron Johnson

Notes

Introduction

1 George Gallup Jr., *Religion in America 1990* (Princeton: Princeton Religion Research Center, 1985); D. Michael Lindsay and George Gallup Jr., *Surveying the American Religious Landscape: Trends in U.S. Beliefs* (New York: Morehouse Group, 2000).

2 Andrew M. Greeley, *The Sociology of the Paranormal: A Reconnaissance* (Beverly Hills, Calif.: Sage, 1975); *Religious Change in America* (Cambridge: Harvard University Press, 1989).

3 Will Herberg, *Protestant–Catholic–Jew* (Garden City, N.Y.: Doubleday, 1960).

4 Robert Lee, *The Social Sources of Church Unity* (New York: Abingdon, 1960).

5 For example, Martin E. Marty, *The New Shape of American Religion* (New York: Harper, 1959).

6 Gerhard Lenski, *The Religious Factor: A Sociological Study of Religion's Impact on Politics, Economics, and Family Life* (Garden City, N.Y.: Doubleday).

7 Stark and Glock, *American Piety*, 25.

8 Calculated on the basis of members per 1,000 U.S. population. See Rodney Stark, *Sociology*, 10th ed. (Belmont, Calif.: Wadsworth, 2007).

9 Robert Wuthnow, *The Restructuring of American Religion* (Princeton: Princeton University Press, 1988), 156.

10 Rodney Stark and Roger Finke, *Acts of Faith: Explaining the Human Side of Religion* (Berkeley: University of California Press, 2000), 121.

11 Robert D. Putnam, *Bowling Alone* (New York: Simon & Schuster, 2000), 70–72.

12 Wuthnow, *Restructuring of American Religion*, 159.

13 See Dean C. Curry, "Evangelical Amnesia," *First Things*, October 1 2007: 15–17.

14 Robert Wuthnow, "Recent Patterns of Secularization: A Problem of Generations?" *American Sociological Review* 41 (1976): 850–67.

15 Wuthnow, *Restructuring of American Religion*, 156.

16 Roger Finke and Rodney Stark, *The Churching of America 1776–1990* (New Brunswick, N.J.: Rutgers University Press, 1991).

17 The Baylor statistic was done differently than the other percentages. After asking people their religious preference, the poll then asked for the name of their current place of worship and where it was located. Sixty-nine percent did so.

18 For a summary see Rodney Stark, *Discovering God: The Origins of the Great Religions and the Evolution of Belief* (San Francisco: Harper One, 2007).

Chapter 1

1 C. Kirk Hadaway, Penny Long Marler, and Mark Chavez, "What the Polls Don't Show: A Closer Look at Church Attendance," *American Sociological Review* 58 (1993): 741–52.

2 Michael Hout and Andrew Greeley, "What Church Officials' Reports Don't Show: Another Look at Church Attendance Data," *American Sociological Review* 63 (1998): 113–19.

3 Laurence R. Iannaccone and Sean F. Everton, "Never on Sunny Days: Lessons from Weekly Attendance Counts," *Journal for the Scientific Study of Religion* 43 (2004): 191–207.

Chapter 2

1 Editorial, *Wall Street Journal*, March 1, 2008: A8.

2 Quoted in Finke and Stark, *Churching of America*, 9.

3 Robin Williams Jr., *American Society* (New York: Knopf, 1951), 312.

4 Peter Berger, *The Sacred Canopy* (New York: Doubleday, 1969).

5 See Harvey Cox, *The Secular City* (New York: Macmillan, 1965).

6   Adam Smith, *An Inquiry into the Nature and Causes of the Wealth of Nations*, vol. 2 [1776], ed. R. H. Campbell and A. S. Skinner (Indianapolis: Liberty Fund, 1981), 793.

7   Gary A. Tobin and Aryeh K. Weinberg, *Profiles of the American University*, vol. 2 (San Francisco: Institute for Jewish & Community Research, 2007).

8   Louis Bolce and Gerald De Maio, "Religious Outlook, Culture War Politics, and Antipathy Toward Christian Fundamentalists," *Public Opinion Quarterly* 63 (1999): 29–61.

9   Quoted in Stark and Finke, *Acts of Faith*, 221.

Chapter 3

1   Benton Johnson, "On Church and Sect," *American Sociological Review* 28 (1963): 539–49.

2   Rodney Stark and William Sims Bainbridge, *The Future of Religion: Secularization, Revival and Cult Formation* (Berkeley: University of California Press, 1985).

3   Laurence Iannaccone, "Sacrifice and Stigma: Reducing Free-Riding in Cults, Communes and Other Collectives," *Journal of Political Economy* 100, no. 2 (1992): 271–91.

Chapter 4

1   D. Michael Lindsay, "A Gated Community in the Evangelical World," *USA Today*, February 11, 2008.

2   Wuthnow, *Restructuring of American Religion*, ch. 6.

3   Edward H. Hammett, *The Gathered and Scattered Church* (Macon, Ga: Smyth & Helwys, 2005).

4   Hammett, *Gathered and Scattered Church*, xi.

5   Hammett, *Gathered and Scattered Church*, 2.

Chapter 5

1   Quoted in Amy C. Sims, "Religion Gets Supersized at Mega-churches," FOXNews.com, February 3, 2004.

2   Quoted in Scott Thumma and Dave Travis, *Beyond Megachurch Myths* (San Francisco: Jossey-Bass, 2007), 21.

3   Sims, "Religion Gets Supersized."

4   The Rapture of the church refers to the idea, expressed in 1 Thessalonians 4:13-18, that believers will be caught up bodily

into heaven at some point during the end times. Beliefs about exactly when the Rapture will take place (before, during, or after the Great Tribulation) vary among denominations.

5   Quoted in Thumma and Travis, *Beyond Megachurch Myths*, 78.

Chapter 6

1   Written and generously paid for by Andrew Greeley.

2   William James, *The Varieties of Religious Experience* (New York: Longmans, Green, 1902).

3   Edwn Diller Starbuck, *The Psychology of Religion* (New York: Scribner's, 1901).

4   Evelyn Underhill, *Mysticism* (London: Methuen, 1911).

Chapter 7

1   For a summary, see Rodney Stark, *The Rise of Christianity* (Princeton: Princeton University Press, 1996), ch. 5.

2   Adolf von Harnack, *The Mission and Expansion of Christianity in the First Three Centuries*, vol. 2 (New York: Putnam's, 1908), 73.

3   Mary Beard, John North, and Simon Price, *Religions of Rome*, vol. 1 (Cambridge: Cambridge University Press, 1998), 297.

4   Rodney Stark, *Exploring the Religious Life* (Baltimore: The Johns Hopkins University Press, 2004), ch. 4.

5   See Stark, *Exploring*, ch. 4.

6   Alan Miller, "Going to Hell in Asia: The Relationship between Risk and Religion in a Cross-Cultural Setting," *Review of Religious Research* 42 (2000): 5–18.

7   Alan Miller and Rodney Stark, "Gender and Religiousness: Can Socialization Explanations Be Saved?" *American Journal of Sociology* 107 (2002): 1399–1423.

Chapter 8

1   Jackson W. Carroll, Douglas W. Johnson, and Martin E. Marty, *Religion in America, 1950 to the Present* (New York: Harper & Row, 1979), 31.

2   Charles Y. Glock and Rodney Stark, *Christian Beliefs and Anti-Semitism* (New York: Harper & Row, 1969).

3   Alan F. Segal, "Heaven, Yes; Hell, Not So Much," On Faith from

www.washingtonpost.com. See also *Life After Death: A History of the Afterlife in the West* (Garden City, N.Y.: Doubleday, 2004).

Chapter 10

1   Jeffrey Burton Russell, *The Prince of Darkness: Radical Evil and the Power of Good in History* (Ithaca: Cornell University Press, 1988).

2   See Michael B. Lupfer, Donna Tolliver, and Mark Jackson, "Explaining Life-Altering Occurrences: A Test of the 'God-of-the-Gaps' Hypothesis," *Journal for the Scientific Study of Religion* 35, no. 4 (1996): 379–91.

3   The genesis for this analogy comes from W. V. Quine and J. S. Ullian, *The Web of Belief* (New York: Random House, 1978), although this philosophical treatise deals with these issues only peripherally, as the epistemological foundations of science are its central concern.

Chapter 11

1   Brian J. Zinnbauer, Kenneth I. Pargament, Brenda Cole, Mark S. Rye, Eric M. Butter, Timothy G. Belavich, Kathleen M. Hipp, Allie B. Scott, Jill L. Kadar, "Religion and Spirituality: Unfuzzying the Fuzzy," *Journal for the Scientific Study of Religion* 36 (1997): 549–64.

2   Wade Clark Roof, *A Generation of Seekers: The Spiritual Journeys of the Baby Boom Generation* (San Francisco: Harper Collins, 1993); Zinnbauer et al., "Religion and Spirituality"; R. O. Scott, "Are You Religious or Are You Spiritual? A Look in the Mirror," *Spirituality and Health* (Spring 2001): 26–28; Robert C. Fuller, *Spiritual, but Not Religious: Understanding Unchurched America* (New York: Oxford University Press, 2001); Penny Long Marler and C. Kirk Hadaway, "'Being Religious' or 'Being Spiritual' in America: A Zero-Sum Proposition?" *Journal for the Scientific Study of Religion* 41 (2002): 289–300.

3   Leila Shahabi, Lynda H. Powell, Marc A. Musick, Kenneth I. Pargament, Carl E. Thoresen, David Williams, Lynn Underwood, and Marcia A. Ory, "Correlates of Self-Perceptions of Spirituality in American Adults," *Annals of Behavioral Medicine* 24 (2002): 59–68.

4   Fuller, *Spiritual, but Not Religious*, 7.

5   Zinnbauer et al., "Religion and Spirituality"; Shahabi et al., "Correlates of Self-Perceptions."

6   Shahabi et al., "Correlates of Self-Perceptions."

7   Roof, *Generation of Seekers*; Zinnbauer et al., "Religion and Spirituality"; Fuller, *Spiritual, but Not Religious*; Stark, *Exploring the Religious Life*.

8   Fuller, *Spiritual, but Not Religious*, 17.

9   Marler and Hadaway, "'Being Religious.'"

10   In the U.S., atheist is a highly stigmatized social status. See Penny Edgell, Joseph Gerteis, and Douglas Hartmann, "Atheists as 'Other,'" *American Sociological Review* 71 (2006): 211–34.

11   Stark, *Exploring the Religious Life*.

Chapter 13

1   Max Weber, *The Sociology of Religion* (Boston: Beacon Press, 1993 [orig. publ. 1922]), 162–63.

2   Brian D'Onofrio, Lindon Eaves, Lenn Murrelle, Hermine Maes, and Bernard Spilka, "Understanding Biological and Social Influences on Religious Affiliation, Attitudes, and Behaviors: A Behavior Genetic Perspective," *Journal of Personality* 67 (1999): 953–84.

3   Lewis Goldberg, "The Structure of Phenotypic Personality Traits," *American Psychologist* 48 (1993): 26–34; Oliver John and Sanjay Srivastava, "The Big-Five Trait Taxonomy: History, Measurement, and Theoretical Perspectives," in *Handbook of Personality: Theory and Research*, 2d ed., ed. Lawrence Pervin and Oliver John (New York: Guilford Press, 1999), 102–39.

4   Gordon Allport, "Personality and Character," *Psychological Bulletin* 18 (1921): 441–55.

5   Gordon Allport and H. S. Odbert, "Trait-Names: A Psycho-lexical Study," *Psychological Monographs* 47 (1936): 1, whole no. 211.

6   Robert McCrae, "The Five-Factor Model: Issues and Applications [Special Issue]," *Journal of Personality* 60, no. 2 (1992).

7   David Schmitt and David Buss, "Sexual Dimensions of Person Description: Beyond or Subsumed by the Big Five?" *Journal of Research in Personality* 34 (2000): 141–77.

8   Michael Ashton, Kibeom Lee, and Lewis Goldberg, "A Hierarchical Analysis of 1,710 English Personality-Descriptive Adjectives," *Journal of Personality and Social Psychology* 87 (2004): 707–21; Robert Emmons, "Religion in the Psychology of Personality: An Introduction,"

Journal of Personality 67 (1000): 873–88; Douglas MacDonald, "Spirituality: Description, Measurement, and Relation to the Five-Factor Model of Personality," *Journal of Personality* 68 (2000): 153–97; Ralph Piedmont, "Does Spirituality Represent the Sixth Factor of Personality? Spiritual Transcendence and the Five-Factor Model. *Journal of Personality* 67 (1999): 985–1014; Vassilis Saroglou, "Religion and the Five Factors of Personality: A Meta-analytic Review," *Personality and Individual Differences* 32 (2002): 15–25.

9   Samuel Gosling, Peter Rentfrow, and William Swann, "A Very Brief Measure of the Big-Five Personality Domains," *Journal of Research in Personality* 37 (2003): 504–28.

10   Saroglou, "Religion and the Five Factors of Personality," 15–25.

11   Russell Eisenman, Jan Grossman, and Ronald Goldstein, "Undergraduate Marijuana Use as Related to Internal Sensation Novelty Seeking and Openness to Experience," *Journal of Clinical Psychology* 36 (1980): 1013–19.

12   Andrew Kohut, John Green, Scott Keeter, and Robert Toth, *The Diminishing Divide* (Washington, D.C.: Brookings Institution Press, 2000).

Chapter 14

1   Stark and Finke, *Acts of Faith*, 57.

2   Max Müller, *Lectures on the Origin and Growth of Religion as Illustrated by the Religions of India* (London: Longmans Green, 1880), 218.

3   Anthony F. C. Wallace, *Religion: An Anthropological View* (New York: Random House, 1966), 264–65.

4   Peter Berger, "A Bleak Outlook Is Seen for Religion," *The New York Times*, April 25, 1968, p. 3.

5   Ariela Keysar, Egon Mayer, and Barry A. Kosmin, "No Religion: A Profile of America's Unchurched," *Public Perspective* 14 (2003): 28–32.

6   Stark, *Exploring the Religious Life*, ch. 6.

7   James R. Kluegel, "Denominational Mobility," *Journal for the Scientific Study of Religion* 19 (1980): 26–39; and Darren E. Sherkat and John Wilson, "Preferences, Constraints, and Choices in Religious Markets," *Social Forces* 73 (1995): 993–1026.

8   Paul Froese, *The Plot to Kill God: Findings from the Soviet Experiment in Secularization* (Berkeley: University of California Press, 2008).

9   H. Allen Orr, review of *The God Delusion* by Richard Dawkins, *New York Review of Books*, January 11, 2007.

10   Terry Eagleton, review of *The God Delusion* by Richard Dawkins, *London Review of Books*, October 2006.

11   Michael Novak, "Remembering the Secular Age," *First Things*, June/July 2007.

12   Richard Cimino and Christopher Smith, "Secular Humanism and Atheism beyond Progressive Secularism," *Sociology of Religion* 68 (2007): 407–24.

13   Alexander Yakovlev, *A Century of Violence in the Soviet Union* (New Haven: Yale University Press, 2002).

Chapter 15

1   William Sims Bainbridge and Rodney Stark, "Superstitions: Old and New," *Skeptical Inquirer* 4 (1980): 18–31.

2   John W. Fox, "The Structure, Stability, and Social Antecedents of Reported Paranormal Experiences," *Sociological Analysis* 53 (1992): 417–31; Erich Goode, *Paranormal Beliefs: A Sociological Introduction* (Prospect Heights, Ill.: Waveland Press, 2000); Tom W. Rice, "Believe It or Not: Religious and Other Paranormal Beliefs in the United States," *Journal for the Scientific Study of Religion* 42, no. 1 (2003): 95–106.

Chapter 16

1   H. Richard Niebuhr, *The Social Sources of Denominationalism* (New York: Henry Holt, 1929), 19.

2   Bernard Lang, *Monotheism and the Prophetic Majority* (Sheffield: The Almond Press, 1983), 68.

3   Stark, *Rise of Christianity*.

4   Rodney Stark, *Discovering God* (San Francisco: Harper One, 2007).

5   Stark, *Discovering God*.

6   J. Gordon Melton, *The Encyclopedia of American Religions*. 7th ed. (Detroit: Gale Cengage, 2002).

7   Stark and Bainbridge, *Future of Religion*, ch. 18.

Chapter 17

1   Keysar, Mayer, and Kosmin, "No Religion," 28–32.

2   Gallup poll in Carroll, Johnson, and Marty, *Religion in America*.

3   See the General Social Surveys.

4   Stark, *Exploring the Religious Life*, ch. 6.

Chapter 18

1   Tobin and Weinberg, *Religious Identity and Behavior of College Faculty*.

2   Harvey Cox, quoted in Kevin Phillips, *American Theocracy* (New York: Penguin Books, 2007).

3   Michelle Goldberg, *Kingdom Coming: The Rise of Christian Nationalism* (New York: W. W. Norton, 2006).

4   Rabbi James Rudin, *The Baptizing of America: The Religious Right's Plans for the Rest of Us* (New York: Thunder Mouth Press, 2006).

5   See Philip Hamburger, *Separation of Church and State* (Cambridge: Harvard University Press, 2002).

6   David Barton, *The Myth of Separation* (Aledo, Tex.: WallBuilder Press, 1993).

7   Paul Blanshard, *American Freedom and Catholic Power* (Boston: Beacon Press, 1958 [orig. publ. 1949]), 346.

Chapter 21

1   Due to low sample sizes, we do not report figures for black Protestant and non-Christian religious groups.

2   Jerry Z. Park and Joseph Baker, "What Would Jesus Buy: American Consumption of Religious and Spiritual Material Goods," *Journal for the Scientific Study of Religion* 46, no. 4 (2007): 501–17.

Chapter 22

1   Robert Bellah, Richard Madsen, William M. Sullivan, Ann Swidler, and Steven M. Tipton, *Habits of the Heart* (Berkeley: University of California Press, 1996 [orig. publ. 1985]), xxxiii.

2   Putnam, *Bowling Alone*.

3   Robert Wuthnow, *Loose Connections: Joining Together in America's Fragmented Communities* (Cambridge: Harvard University Press, 1998).

4   Christopher Jencks, "Who Gives to What?" in *The Nonprofit Sector: A Research Handbook*, ed. W. W. Powell (New Haven: Yale University Press, 1987).

Chapter 23

1   John P. Bartkowski, Xiaohe Xu, and Martin L. Levin, "Religion and Child Development: Evidence from the Early Childhood Longitudinal Study," *Social Science Research* 37, no. 1 (2008): 18–36.

2   Rajeev H. Dehejia, Thomas DeLeire, Erzo F. P. Luttmer, and Joshua Mitchell, "The Role of Religious and Social Organizations in the Lives of Disadvantaged Youth," NBER Working Paper No. W13369 (September 2007); Linda D. Loury, "Does Church Attendance Really Increase Schooling?" *Journal for the Scientific Study of Religion* 43, no. 1 (2004): 119–27.

3   See Dehejia, et al., "Role of Religious and Social Organizations."

4   The high-education occupations are business, science/architecture/engineering/computers, community/social service, legal, education, arts/design/entertainment/sports/media, and health care practitioner/technician. The mid-range -education occupations are health care support, protective service, personal care/service, sales, office/administrative support, farming/fishing/forestry, installation/repair, and law enforcement. The low-education occupations are food preparation and serving, building/grounds cleaning/maintenance, construction/extraction, transportation/material moving, military, manufacturing, and homemaker.

Contributors

Christopher Bader, associate professor of sociology; **Joseph Baker**, graduate student in sociology; **Kevin Dougherty**, assistant professor of sociology; **Scott Draper**, graduate student, sociology; **Robyn Driskell**, associate dean of arts & sciences; **Paul Froese,** assistant professor of sociology; **Carl R. Gwin**, associate professor of economics, Pepperdine University; **Sung Joon Jang**, associate professor of sociology; **Byron Johnson**, professor of sociology and codirector, Institute for Studies of Religion; **Megan Johnson**, graduate student in psychology; **Jordan LaBouff**, graduate student in psychology; **Larry Lyon**, dean of the graduate school; **Carson Mencken**, professor of sociology; **Charles M. North**, associate professor of economics; **Wafa Hakim Orman**, post-doctoral fellow in economics; **Ashley Palmer-Boyes**, graduate student in sociology; **Jerry Z. Park**, assistant professor of sociology; **Wade Rowatt**, associate professor of psychology.

All contributors except Carl Gwin are at Baylor.